Digital Payments in India

Background, Trends and Opportunities

By

Jaspal Singh (IPS),
Inspector General of Police, Goa

New Century Publications
New Delhi, India

New Century Publications
4852 / 24, 1st Floor,
Ansari Road, Daryaganj,
New Delhi – 110 002 (India)

Tel.: 011-4101 7798; 4358 7398; 98112 66355
E-mail: info@newcenturypublications.com

www.newcenturypublications.com

Editorial office:
4800 / 24, Bharat Ram Road,
Ansari Road, Daryaganj,
New Delhi – 110 002

Edition: 2026

ISBN: **978-81-7708-492-4**

First Published: 2019

Published by New Century Publications and printed at Milan Enterprises, New Delhi.

Designs: Patch Creative Unit, New Delhi.

PRINTED IN INDIA

About the Book

Payment systems form the backbone of an economy. The spectacular growth in financial transactions has necessitated certain radical changes in the payment systems around the world. The technological revolution in the field of electronics and telecommunications has helped to bring about sophisticated developments in the payment systems in many countries. What seemed futuristic a couple of decades ago is pedestrian now. A well-defined payment system is, therefore, a crucial component of the financial infrastructure of a country.

India has been enjoying a very healthy evolution of payment systems. This has been the result of a calibrated approach adopted by the Reserve Bank of India—in the initial years as a developer, and in later years as a catalyst and facilitator. Presently, India's payment systems are not only comparable to systems anywhere in the world, but are standards for other emerging economies to emulate.

According to a survey conducted by The Economist Intelligence Unit for the year 2018, India is taking rapid strides in advancing e-payment capabilities and is one of the top-performing countries in terms of citizen-to-government (C2G), business-to-government (B2G) and government-to-business (G2B) transactions.

In the 73-country survey, India's overall ranking on the government's adoption of e-payments moved up to 28th in 2018, from 36th in 2011. The country holds top ranking on B2G and G2B, and comes third on C2G, jointly with Argentina.

National Payments Corporation of India (NPCI) is the mainstay of payment systems and its proximate objective is to provide convenient *anytime-anywhere* payment services that are secure and easy-to-use.

Not many people and organizations, both within the country and abroad, are aware of the payment systems existing in India. This book is an informative and descriptive document on the subject.

About the Author

Shri Jaspal Singh (IPS) is currently Inspector General of Police, Goa. He joined the Indian Police Service in 1996 and has served in Delhi, Goa, Puducherry and Andaman and Nicobar (A&N) Islands in various capacities. He has handled field assignments for 12 years in different ranks.

He is the recipient of the Police Medal for Meritorious Service, Police Medal for Hard Duty and Lt. Governor's Commendation for exemplary work in A&N Islands during the massive earthquake and Tsunami.

While still a student, he was nominated as a member of the University Senate by the Governor of Punjab for his excellence in academics.

Shri Jaspal graduated with Honours in Economics from Guru Nanak Dev University (GNDU), Amritsar, Punjab and holds a law degree from University of Delhi, Delhi. He also holds a Post-graduate degree in Management from GNDU, Amritsar, Punjab and a Masters degree in Computer Applications from Indira Gandhi National Open University (IGNOU), New Delhi. He was also a faculty member of the Department of Business Management, GNDU, Amritsar, Punjab. He also served as a senior executive with state-owned Hindustan Petroleum Corporation Limited.

He has received training with the Police Department of Los Angeles (US) and also attended a course organized by the US Department of State on Advanced Explosive Incident Counter Measures.

Shri Jaspal has also compiled a book titled *Aman Ka Gehwara*.

Contents

Preface

Payments system provides the arteries or highways for conducting trade, commerce and other forms of economic activities in any country. An efficient payments system functions as a lubricant speeding up the liquidity flow in the economy and creating a momentum for economic growth. The payments process is a vital aspect of financial intermediation; it enables the creation and transfer of liquidity among different economic agents. A smooth, well-functioning payments system not only ensures efficient utilisation of scarce resources but also eliminates systemic risks.

Payments system assumes importance in the context of domestic financial sector reforms and global financial integration. The time value of money flows has increased sharply in view of the competing demands on the financial sector. Efficient, low cost cross-border payments flow helps to promote international trade in goods and services. Foreign investments (direct and portfolio) are encouraged by the availability of an efficient payments system. For these reasons, an efficient and technologically advanced payments and settlement system performs a vital infrastructural function in the economy. Reserve Bank of India (RBI) has, therefore, been taking measures to set up such an infrastructural set up.

The payment instruments are constantly changing and newer products and services are being innovated in the developed and developing countries and these are being introduced with suitable modifications and safeguards in India. At the retail level, a wide range of payment instruments are catering to the needs of different types of economic transactions. At the level of inter-bank payments and settlements, real time and online funds transfer are likely to play a major role both in local as well as inter-city dealings.

The experience of computerisation of clearing operations as well as the small beginnings in electronic payments and electronic banking has revealed the need for expansion and upgradation of technology. Still, the development of the payments system is not just a matter of technology. It requires high availability of reliable communication network, the integration of work processes, and delivery systems.

The spread and the reach of the modern system should enable equal and convenient access from both small and big centres alike. The design of an integrated system should be such that there is a wide choice of payments instruments at the retail level and there is end-to-end connectivity over all parts of the country to enable delivery of these instruments through fast, reliable and secure communications.

An integrated system would enable real time movement of funds between different financial markets, allow fair and equal access to all the financial intermediaries and enable effective regulatory oversight. The fundamental requirement is the integration of various payments instruments, transactions and settlements into a single system which combines flexibility with efficiency. This would have implications for not merely seigniorage but also the conduct of monetary policy.

Managing data security and privacy will remain a priority for policymakers. Given varying degrees of discomfort with government surveillance around the world, different jurisdictions will approach regulation in different ways. This could lead to some regulatory arbitrage as fintechs seek out less onerous regulatory regimes. The more radical e-payment innovations—for instance, those incorporating facial recognition technology—could emerge in countries such as China, where citizens seem to be more tolerant of potential privacy intrusions.

The global e-payments ecosystem will continue to evolve at a staggering pace, as traditional concepts of finance, personal identity and trust are upended almost overnight by technological advances. Governments have been trying to strike a balance between e-payments' promise—for instance, increased efficiency in tax collection and social services expenditure—and their possible risks.

Digital India (DI): Vision 2019 is an initiative of the

Government of India to integrate Government Ministries and Departments with the people of India. It aims at ensuring the availability of government services to citizens electronically by reducing paperwork. The initiative also includes plans to connect rural areas with high-speed internet networks. DI has three core components. These include creation of digital infrastructure, delivering services digitally and digital literacy.

Cyber space is vulnerable to a wide variety of incidents, whether intentional or accidental, man-made or natural, and the data exchanged in the cyber space can be exploited for nefarious purposes by both nation-states and non-state actors. Cyber attacks that target the infrastructure or underlying economic well-being of a nation-state can effectively reduce available state resources and undermine confidence in their supporting structures.

National Cyber Security Policy (NCSP), 2013, was a policy framework by Department of Electronics and Information Technology (DeitY), Ministry of Communication and Information Technology, Government of India. It aimed at protecting the public and private infrastructure from cyber attacks. The policy also intends to safeguard "information, such as personal information (of web users), financial and banking information and sovereign data". This was particularly relevant in the wake of US National Security Agency (NSA) leaks that suggested the US government agencies are spying on Indian users, who have no legal or technical safeguards against it.

Crypto currency—another area of concern—is a class of privately issued digital means of payment that depends predominantly on cryptography and distributed ledger technology (DLT) such as the block chain. A block chain is a continuous ledger in which transactions are stored as blocks and linked using cryptography. Crypto currency is often allotted through initial coin offerings (ICOs), which are used as a means of raising capital through crowd-funding. Crypto currency typically has some monetary characteristics, but is not a liability of any entity and is not backed by any authority. Its value is driven by users' confidence in it. This, coupled with limited supply, makes its value highly volatile and, therefore, not a reliable medium of exchange or store of value.

Though crypto currency may not currently pose systemic risks, its increasing popularity leading to price bubbles raises serious concerns for consumer and investor protection, and market integrity.

Governments, private-sector firms and non-governmental organisations, sensing that traditional banking models are evolving and disintermediated, are competing and collaborating in equal measure as they vie for influence in this new age of digital finance.

Acknowledgements

This work draws, in part, on the information provided in the publications and websites of various national and international institutions/organizations, in particular the Ministry of Finance, Government of India, Ministry of Communications and Information Technology, Government of India, Reserve Bank of India (RBI), National Payments Corporation of India (NPCI), and NITI Aayog. Use of information from these sources is gratefully acknowledged.

Goa **Jaspal Singh**

1

Role of Payment Systems and India's Current E-payments Ranking

Under a system of simple commodity production, exchange of goods was accomplished largely through barter. The main difficulty of the barter system was the double coincidence of wants. In a modern economy, characterised by acute specialisation and exchange, barter system would just be impossible. It is, therefore, necessary to accept some one thing as a medium of exchange. Any generally accepted thing which serves as a medium of exchange may be called money. Historically, a variety of things have served as money including goats, coins, paper currency and demand deposits of banks.

The first and the most important function of money is to act as a medium of exchange. As a matter of fact, money is defined in terms of this unique function. Other functions of money are more or less derived from this function. By using money as a medium of exchange, a society can get rid of the difficulties of barter system. By the use of money, exchange becomes easy and this promotes specialisation which has its own advantages in a modern society.

1.1 Money and Payment Obligations

Use of money for settlement of payment obligations has a very long history. Use of non-cash exchange through barter preceded the introduction of money. Barter, however, co-exists with monetised economy in some underdeveloped agricultural societies even now. But currency or cash is the most readily accepted medium of exchange in all modern societies because it is the legal tender and helps to bring about irrevocable settlement.

There are, however, certain disadvantages associated with the use of cash. Holding cash does not fetch any return-the interest foregone because of cash holding is a cost to the holder of cash. Besides, the holder of cash bears some insurance costs in terms of the premiums that are paid to cover any loss/theft. Moreover, carrying of large quantities of cash to make large-value payments is a security risk and also involves transportation costs.

Payment and settlement systems form the backbone of any economy. The spectacular growth in financial transactions has necessitated certain radical changes in the payments and settlement systems around the globe. The technological revolution in the field of electronics and telecommunications has helped to bring about sophisticated developments in the payments and settlement systems in many countries. A well defined payments and settlement system is, therefore, a crucial component of the financial infrastructure of any country.

Payments system provides the arteries or highways for conducting trade, commerce and other forms of economic activities in any country. An efficient payments system functions as a lubricant speeding up the liquidity flow in the economy and creating a momentum for economic growth. The payments process is a vital aspect of financial intermediation; it enables the creation and transfer of liquidity among different economic agents. A smooth, well-functioning payments system not only ensures efficient utilisation of scarce resources but also eliminates systemic risks.

Payments system assumes importance in the context of domestic financial sector reforms and global financial integration. The time value of money flows has increased sharply in view of the competing demands on the financial sector. Efficient, low cost cross-border payments flow helps to promote international trade in goods and services. Foreign investments (direct and portfolio) are encouraged by the availability of an efficient payments system. For these reasons, an efficient and technologically advanced payments and settlement system performs a vital infrastructural function in the economy. Reserve Bank of India (RBI) has, therefore, been taking measures to set up such an infrastructural set up.

1.2 Importance of a Sound Payment System

The payment and settlement systems are at the core of financial infrastructure in a country. A well-functioning payment and settlement system is crucial for the successful implementation of monetary policy and maintaining the financial stability. Central banks have, therefore, always maintained a keen interest in the development of payment and settlement system as part of their responsibilities for monetary and financial stability. In India, the development of a safe, secure and sound payment and settlement system has been the key policy objective. In this direction, the RBI, apart from performing the regulatory and supervisory functions, has also been making efforts to promote functionality and modernisation of the payment and settlement systems on an ongoing basis.

A safe and efficient payment system is a prerequisite for smooth functioning of the financial markets. The conduct of monetary policy in an effective manner requires safe and efficient payment and settlement systems to facilitate transfer of funds and securities between the central bank and other participants in the financial system. An efficient and stable payment and settlement system is also a pre-condition for inter-bank money markets and other short-term credit markets through which monetary policy is transmitted. In addition, developments in the payment and settlement systems that affect the speed and realisation/availability of funds for further deployment can influence the overall demand for money in the economy.

By linking financial institutions together for the purpose of transferring monetary claims and settling payment obligations, payment and settlement system becomes a channel through which financial risks are transmitted across financial institutions and markets. Well-designed and efficiently managed systems, therefore, help in maintaining financial stability by reducing uncertainty of settlement. Settlement failures which spread to other payment and settlement systems through the contagion effect not only undermine the smooth functioning of the financial markets, but can also adversely affect the public confidence in money and efficacy of the instruments used to transfer money.

Payment and settlement systems, which constitute the backbone of the financial economy, aim at minimising the systemic risk. The payment system influences the speed, financial risk, reliability and the cost of domestic and international transactions. With the significant improvements in payment and settlement systems, depth and liquidity of various segments of the financial market can be improved.

Settlement systems in India have evolved over a period of time from physical settlement systems with considerable amount of risks to the current electronic systems with central counterparty with emphasis on risk mitigation. During the early 1990s, government securities market was opaque with limited information dissemination and inefficient pricing. The securities were held in physical form requiring execution of physical transfer forms for transfer of securities in any trade leading to inefficiencies in settling the trades. Settlement of securities and funds legs were independent of each other (non-DvP), leading to considerable settlement risks. Moreover, pre-settlement comparison and confirmation of trades was not systematised. Settlement cycles were not uniform with settlements happening on T+0 and T+1 basis.

1.3 Forms of Payments

The requirements of a modern economy in regard to settlement of transactions are diverse and variegated and the needs of manufacturing, trade, and commerce activities involve large value payments over vast geographic distances. External trade with the rest of the world involves payments in different currencies. Payments can no longer be completed by simple cash transfer in such cases. Therefore, there arises the need for additional forms of payments, which can be facilitated with improved financial intermediation and expansion of financial instruments. Cheques and other paper-based instruments and to some extent electronic instruments have become important modes of payment in recent times in most countries because of growing financial intermediation.

Individuals, business entities or governments issue cheques or other forms of order on their banks in discharge of their payment obligations. The recipients of these orders would then get the funds embodied in these payment instruments through their own banks. As the number of banks grew over time, the volume of instruments exchanged among them increased substantially. Consequently, as also to have an orderly means of transfer of payment instructions among banks at a location or centre, a common set of practices and mechanisms of exchange had to be evolved. When instruments presented by customers of banks become payable at outside locations, special collection arrangements are set in motion to collect the funds. If the collecting bank has a branch at the relevant outside location, there would be no problem, but, if the collecting bank does not have a branch at the outside location, it will have to enter into correspondent banking relationship with another bank at the said outside location for the purpose of collecting funds.

The payment instruments which are routed through financial intermediaries involve book entries at various levels to transfer funds from one party to the other. The range of intermediation varies to take care of different situations. This may, for instance, consist of instructions to intermediaries to move goods coinciding with the movement of funds as in the case of a letter of credit. Or, the instruction could be for payment of specified sums of money to the bearer of a payment instrument, as in the case of a bearer cheque. In some cases, the payment instruments are negotiable in the sense that they can be transferred from person to person in lieu of cash. In yet other cases, both the ultimate beneficiary and the destination could be pre-determined. In all these cases, banks play a crucial part in conveying, transmitting and carrying out the instructions embodied in the payment instruments.

While doing so, these intermediaries have to settle among themselves the monetary claims arising from the execution of payment instructions. Thus, whenever non-cash payment instruments are involved, they are accompanied by a chain of related fund transfers as well as a stream of book entries and messages. Banks in turn need an intermediate agency such as the clearing house where these instruments can be exchanged and where the financial claims on one another can be settled through a settlement bank, which is usually the central bank of the country.

Clearing houses facilitate the exchange of instruments and processing of payment instructions at a central point among the participating banks. Clearing houses—manual and paper based—in many advanced countries have gradually extended their range of activities to include automated and electronic means for settlement of payment transactions. Such an evolution is also seen in emerging economies.

Banks, as crucial intermediaries in the payments stream, provide deposit accounts to non bank agents (i.e. individuals, firms/corporate bodies) which are considered as liquid assets and facilitate payments transactions. Banks provide credit facilities so that such payments can be effected with lower working balances. Moreover, they act as conduit through which domestic and international capital markets provide resources to the commercial sector.

1.4 India's Payment System Architecture

Payment system architecture in India is based on international benchmarks, and guiding principles. The Payment and Settlement System Act, 2007, provides a comprehensive legal framework for payment and settlement services in India for subjects like authorisation of payment system operators, netting and finality of payment and settlement. The payment system objectives of having a safe, sound, cost-effective and wide distribution network are being met in so far as the large value and countrywide payment and settlement systems are concerned. The grand vision is that cash dominant economy may transit to a predominantly non-cash dominant economy with non-cash transactions primarily in electronic mode, which is the international norm. The existing payment system is being constantly reviewed to suggest an action plan for orderly growth of the payment systems.

Since 2015-16, all segments of electronic payments, particularly retail electronic payments, have shown healthy growth both in terms of volume and value of usage. For example, real time gross settlement (RTGS) and national electronic funds transfer (NEFT) value registered a growth of 41 percent and 107 percent respectively between 2015-16 and 2017-2018, reflecting greater adoption of the system by all segments of users. Similarly, with increasing number of banks offering mobile banking services and driven by the growth in e-commerce and use of mobile payment applications, the volume of mobile banking transactions witnessed a growth of 92 percent for the period 2016-17 to 2017-18.

Card transactions have also grown significantly at both ATMs as well as at the point-of-sale (PoS) with the growth in debit card usage at PoS picking up significantly. The growth in volume and value of transactions using pre-paid payment instruments (PPIs) issued by banks and authorised non-bank entities has also been significant. The volume and value in immediate payment service (IMPS) has also grown significantly with the development of the IMPS as a multi-channel system providing various options to customers to originate transactions. Paper clearing, on the other hand, witnessed a marginal growth of 6.7 percent in terms of volume between 2015 and 2018.

Payment systems in India comprise electronic payment systems as well as paper-based systems. Another classification pertains to large value payment systems and retail payment systems.

1.4.1 Large Value Payment Systems: The large value payment infrastructure comprises RTGS, high value clearing, and CCIL. Based on the criteria outlined by CPSS, the RTGS system and the high value clearing system have been identified as SIPS. The funds leg of the CCIL-operated clearing systems covering government securities, foreign exchange and money market settle in the RTGS system.

The Indian RTGS system was operationalised in March 2004. The system started operations with four banks and settled only inter-bank transactions. Subsequently, the system was opened for settlement of customer transactions. It was operationalised for settlement of multilateral net settlement batch (MNSB) files from September 2006.

RTGS system is owned and operated by the Reserve Bank of India (RBI). The system works on a mainframe computer. Members are provided with a participant interface (PI), using which the participants connect to the system at the RBI through the INFINET. The message flow architecture in the RTGS system uses the Y topology. The members communicate through their PI to the inter-bank funds transfer processor (IFTP) which validates all communication and also does the *strip and store* function.

Upon successful completion of a transaction and receipt of confirmation from the RTGS, the IFTP forwards the complete credit information to the beneficiary member's PI. All communication between the PI and IFTP and IFTP to RTGS uses digital signatures (public key infrastructure) to ensure security.

The membership of RTGS is open to all scheduled commercial banks (SCBs), primary dealers (PDs) and others, as may be decided by the RBI. The SCBs are provided with Type A membership, primary dealers Type B and clearing houses Type D membership.

Except Type A members, customer-based transactions cannot be submitted by other members. Type D members are permitted to submit only net settlement batches for settlement under the RTGS system. Other banks and financial institutions can participate as customers of the direct members.

RTGS operations are governed by the RTGS Membership Regulations, 2004 and RTGS (Membership) Business Operating Guidelines, 2004. The members of the system agree to abide by these regulations and guidelines and any subsequent amendments to these documents.

The settlement of RTGS transactions takes place in the books of the RBI. For this purpose, members have to open a 'RTGS Settlement Account' with the RBI at Mumbai. This account is to be funded at the beginning of each RTGS processing day from the member's current account with the RBI, and at the end of the day, the balance in the settlement account is transferred back to the current account of the member.

Members are provided with collateralized intra-day liquidity (IDL) facility to tide over their IDL mis-matches. This facility is provided to Type A and Type B members only. The IDL facility utilised by the members has to necessarily be reversed by them at the end of RTGS day. Failure to do so attracts penal action.

In addition to IDL, the system provides many features for effective liquidity management by the members. These include message release method, queuing management and queue visibility. The Indian RTGS has adopted the FIFO rule for queuing. The system has a centralised queuing arrangement with priorities assigned by the system participant. The participant and system operator can change the priority of messages/revoke the messages in the queue. The system operator would alter the queue only in extreme situations. At the end of the day, all pending unsettled messages are cancelled by the system. The system has a multilateral offsetting algorithm to resolve any gridlock situations that may arise. This process can be configured to be invoked manually or automatically by the system. Since it is mainly a large-value funds transfer system, a floor of ₹ 2 lakh has been prescribed for minimum value of transactions that can be settled through RTGS.

There has been a substantial increase in the volume of transactions settled through RTGS. The inter-bank clearing at all the RBI centres have been migrated to the RTGS system. Further, multilateral net settlements from CCIL, viz. rupee leg of US dollar-Indian rupee settlement, funds leg of government securities settlement and funds leg of CBLO, and the retail net settlement systems operated by National Clearing Cell, Mumbai (MICR cheque clearing, high value clearing, NEFT and ECS) are settled in RTGS as MNSB files. The liquidity management operations of the RBI are also settled through the RTGS system.

1.4.2 Retail Payment Systems: These include MICR/non-MICR cheque clearing, NEFT system, electronic clearing service (ECS), cheque truncation system (CTS) and payment channels like credit/debit cards, internet and mobile phone-based products.

For details of retail payment systems, see chapters 5 and 6 of this book.

1.5 India's E-payment Ranking in Global Survey

According to the 2018 survey by The Economist Intelligence Unit, commissioned by payments company Visa, India is taking rapid strides in advancing government e-payments capabilities and is one of the top-performing countries in terms of citizen-to-government (C2G), business-to-government (B2G) and government-to-business (G2B) transactions. The country holds the top ranking on B2G and G2B, and comes third on C2G jointly with Argentina.

In the 73-country survey, India's overall ranking on the government's adoption of e-payments [1] moved up to 28th in 2018, from 36th in 2011.

The survey looks at availability of government electronic transaction services and the underlying environment of mechanisms that support digitization for all transactions in a market, such as policy and infrastructure.

According to the survey, India can further improve its standing by focusing on expanding access to digital infrastructure, investing in socio-economic development, and promoting a healthy, competitive market.

The 2018 Government E-Payments Adoption Ranking (GEAR) is an Economist Intelligence Unit (EIU) global index and benchmarking study commissioned by Visa. This is the third edition of the study. The first and second editions were published in 2007 and 2011, respectively.

The objective of the study is to measure the extent to which countries enable payment services on electronic platforms. This includes the availability of government transaction services, and the underlying factors that affect e-payments adoption, such as policy and infrastructure. The overall score and category scores in this benchmarking index are on a normalised scale of 0-100 and represent how countries rank against one another.

The 2018 GEAR study captures some of the essential changes occurring in the worlds of finance and technology, on which developed countries could focus their efforts to advance their government e-payment systems.

The 7 categories and 45 indicators researched in the 2018 GEAR survey are listed in Table 1.1.

The first four pillars of the index examine the availability of certain government payment services. These measure the availability of e-payment facilities, and not whether they are actually used.

The other three pillars—infrastructure, social and economic context and policy context—examine the underlying factors that affect adoption of those e-payment facilities. It is worth reiterating that the transaction services focused on here are government e-payments (where the state is either a payer or a payee), which is a segment of the much broader payments universe.

1.5.1 Overall Rankings: The overall rankings and scores for the 73 countries in the study are presented in Table 1.2. The overall score is a weighted sum of category scores (on a 0-100 scale where 100 is the most favourable). The overall scores reflect the enabling environment for government e-payments adoption.

Table 1.1: Categories and Indicators of the E-payments Survey

1	**Citizen-to-Government (C2G) [2]**
1.1	Payments platform functionality for transaction services
1.2	Income tax payments
1.3	Pension contributions
1.4	Obtaining/paying for an ID card
1.5	Private transit costs
1.6	Public transit payments
2	**Government-to-Citizen (G2C) [3]**
2.1	Income tax refunds
2.2	Pension benefits
2.3	Unemployment benefits
2.4	Government social safety net
3	**Business-to-Government (B2G) [4]**
3.1	Business income tax payments
3.2	VAT/sales tax payments
3.3	Business pension contributions
3.4	Company registration and payment of fees
4	**Government-to-Business (G2B) [5]**
4.1	Business income tax refunds
4.2	VAT/sales tax refunds
4.3	Payments for goods and services
4.4	Disbursement of loans
5	**Infrastructure**
5.1.1	Fixed-line broadband subscribers
5.1.2	Active mobile broadband subscribers
5.1.3	Mobile subscribers
5.1.4	Network coverage (minimum 4G)
5.1.5	Government initiatives to make wi-fi available
5.1.6	Existence of national digital identification system
5.2.1	Automatic teller machines (ATMs) per 10,000 people

contd...

5.2.2	Point-of-sale (POS) terminals per 10,000 people
5.2.3	Development of contactless payments
6	**Social and Economic Context**
6.1.1	Educational attainment
6.1.2	Internet access
6.2.1	Population using banks/other financial institutions
6.2.2	Percentage of firms with a bank loan/line of credit
6.3.1	Proportion of businesses placing orders via the internet
6.3.2	Internet shoppers as a percentage of internet users
6.3.3	Percentage of population with debit card(s)
6.3.4	Used a mobile phone or the internet to access an account
7	**Policy Context**
7.1.1	Fair competition in the payments industry
7.1.2	Policy on acceptance and usage of e-payments
7.1.3	Protection of intellectual property rights
7.1.4	Access to jurisdictions
7.1.5	Government support for FinTech innovation
7.2.1	Government commitment to e-payments security
7.2.2	Government commitment to the Financial Action Task Force (FATF)
7.3.1	Government commitment to integrating the informal economy
7.3.2	Existence of government e-inclusion strategy
7.3.3	Government commitment to financial inclusion

Table 1.2: Overall Ranking and Scores of Top Ten Countries Plus India, China and Pakistan

Rank	Country	Score
1.	Norway	89.7
2.	France	89.4
3.	Denmark	88.8
4.	Canada	88.6

contd...

5.	Australia	88.1
6.	United Kingdom	87.9
7.	South Korea	87.7
8.	Singapore	87.6
9.	Finland	86.2
10.	Sweden	85.8
28.	India	73.3
48.	China	62.4
64.	Pakistan	47.0

Source: Economist Intelligence Unit, *Government E-payments Adoption Ranking Report, September 2018*, p. 17 (excerpted).

1.5.2 Other Main Findings of the Survey: These are as under:

- Government E-payments Adoption Ranking (GEAR) shows that most governments are prioritising the availability of electronic transaction services for citizens and businesses, albeit at different levels, but that they have significant work to do in improving three areas that support e-payments adoption, namely infrastructure, social and economic context, and policy.
- The operating environment for government e-payments has changed significantly in the past decade, and there is much room for growth in terms of availability of services and efficiency. The global payments ecosystem is almost unrecognisable from that which existed at the time of the last GEAR in 2011, particularly in terms of the worldwide growth that has taken place in the availability of e-payment mechanisms.
- While few developing countries feature at the top of the rankings, the seminal trend of these past few years is the continued leapfrogging to more advanced platforms and technologies by emerging markets.
- Developed countries, on the other hand, where many advances in technology and transaction services have already reached completion, can focus on boosting

adoption of systems that have already been enabled while also improving user experiences. At the same time, they need to decide which of the multitude of available new technologies they wish to experiment with. Blockchain-based identity verification and transactions, for instance, appear promising, but it is unclear whether their marginal short-term benefits will justify significant investments, particularly for cash-strapped governments.

- Although it may seem that technology's democratising and decentralising forces are liberating individuals to operate beyond the ambit of the state, the reality is that government policy has never been more important. Countries with proactive governments are the ones that are fostering an enabling environment for fintechs, ensuring financial inclusion and, more generally, striking the appropriate balance between regulatory oversight and unbridled innovation.
- Government e-payment systems have evolved significantly since the first GEAR study in 2007, and yet in some ways the journey is just beginning.

Endnotes

1. E-payments are defined as the exchange or transfer of funds over an electronic payment system. Payments through these electronic platforms can be made by various means, including but not limited to payment card, e-wallet, direct deposit, direct debit, electronic funds transfer and wire transfer. The payment component is only one part of the e-payments process, which can also include online submission of forms and the provision of online instructions or calculators to facilitate the use of an e-payments system.
   Electronic IDs refer to secure digital identifications provided to individuals as part of a national digital identification system or programme. Examples may include biometric enrolment, microprocessor-based smart card technologies or a username or password for online government portals, among other electronic identification-related technologies.
2. **Citizen-to-Government (C2G):** Citizens make regular payments to the state either to fulfil obligations, such as taxes, or to purchase

optional public services, including transportation. This category captures the extent to which citizens can complete these various transactions electronically by assessing six indicators: online one-stop shops; income tax payments; pension contributions; obtaining/paying for an ID card; private transit costs (a composite of automotive tolls, fines, vehicle registration and public parking); and public transit payments.

3. **Government-to-Citizen (G2C):** Governments need to make regular payments to certain segments of the population to fulfil core responsibilities such as providing a social safety net. This category captures the extent to which various government transfers to citizens can be completed electronically, by assessing four indicators: income tax refunds, pension benefits, unemployment benefits and the government social safety net.
4. **Business-to-Government (B2G):** Businesses typically make payments to the state for one of three reasons: to fulfil national obligations, such as taxes; as a form of indirect payment to their employees, such as pension contributions; or for direct business costs, including licence fees. The B2G category captures the extent to which businesses can complete these various transactions electronically by assessing four indicators: income tax payments, value-added/sales tax payments, pension contributions, and company registration and payment of fees.
5. **Government-to-Business (G2B):** The state typically makes payments to businesses for one of three reasons: to refund excessive tax collection, to pay for goods and services purchased, or to disburse small grants or loans to spur business activity. This category captures the extent to which various government transfers to businesses can be completed electronically, by assessing four indicators: income tax refunds, VAT/sales tax refunds, payments for goods and services, and the disbursement of loans.

2

Evolution of Payment Systems in India

2.1 Pre-Independence Payment Systems

The Paper Currency Act of 1861 conferred upon the Government of India the monopoly of note issue bringing to an end note issues of private and Presidency Banks.

In 1881, the Negotiable Instruments Act (NI Act) was enacted, formalising the usage and characteristics of instruments like the cheque, the bill of exchange and promissory note. The NI Act provided a legal framework for non-cash paper payment instruments in India.

With the steady growth in volumes of trade and commerce and the growing confidence of the public in the usage of cheques etc., transactions through the use of these payment instruments grew at a rapid pace. With the development of the banking system and higher turnover in the volume of cheques, the need for an organised cheque clearing process emerged amongst the banks. Clearing associations were formed by the banks in the Presidency towns and the final settlement between member banks was effected by means of cheques drawn upon the Presidency Banks. With the setting up of the Imperial Bank in 1921, settlement was done through cheques drawn on that bank.

The Calcutta Clearing Banks' Association, which was the largest bankers' association at that time, adopted clearing house rules in 1938. The association had twenty-five large banks as its members and eight sub-members. There were two ordinary clearings on each business day, except on Saturday when there was one clearing. However, the association did not cover many banks functioning in Calcutta. The cheques, drafts etc. of such non-clearing banks were collected by the clearing banks only on payment of charges. This affected their business prospects adversely, as the public was not likely to maintain accounts with banks whose cheques suffered a serious handicap of market acceptability.

To overcome this problem, these banks formed themselves into a group called the Metropolitan Banking Association with fifty members, which conducted the Metropolitan Clearing House, in 1939. This association arrived at an understanding with the Calcutta Clearing House in 1940. In addition, two other clearings were conducted in Calcutta: Pioneer clearing and the Walks Clearing.

The Bombay Clearing House was the only association to conduct clearings in Bombay. It had no parallel systems and institutions comparable to the Metropolitan Clearing House of Calcutta. The uniform procedures and charges for collection of non-clearing banks' cheques, drafts, dividend warrants etc. were adopted by the Bombay Clearing House in 1941-42.

After the setting up of Reserve Bank of India under the RBI Act 1935, the clearing houses in the Presidency towns were taken over by the Reserve Bank of India.

2.2 Characteristics of Payment Instruments in India

Negotiable Instruments (NI) Act, 1881, defines a negotiable instrument as a promissory note, bill of exchange or cheque. A bill of exchange is an instrument in writing containing an unconditional order, signed by the maker, directing a certain person to pay a certain sum of money only to, or to the order of, a certain person or to the bearer of the instrument. A *hundi* is a bill of exchange in an Indian language, governed by customs and local usage. The NI Act, however, does not govern *hundis*. A bill of exchange may therefore, include a *hundi*, but *hundi* may not be a bill of exchange.

2.2.1 Cheque: A cheque is a bill of exchange drawn on a specified banker and not expressed to be payable otherwise than on demand. The maker of a cheque is called the *drawer*, and the person directed to pay is the *drawee*. The person named in the instrument, to whom or to whose order the money is, by the instrument directed, to be paid, is called the *payee.* A cheque is a negotiable instrument, which can be further negotiated by means of endorsement and is payable on demand. A cheque payable to bearer is negotiable by the delivery thereof, and when it is payable to order is negotiable by the holder by endorsement and delivery thereof. A cheque has to be presented for payment by the payee or holder to the acceptor, maker or drawer. A cheque payment is a debit transaction as the transaction regarding the payment of a cheque is initiated by the payee or beneficiary.

A cheque is not cash, as it does not assume the finality of payment. The funds may not be available with the drawer or the drawer may have withdrawn funds from his bank account in the interim leading to the possibility of the cheque being dishonoured on presentation. In addition, the banks levy a collection charge based on postal costs as well as the value of the cheque in case of outstation cheques. It takes time to realise the proceeds of a cheque payment, especially if the cheque is an outstation one. For these reasons, the cheque is not always acceptable in several business transactions particularly where the drawer and the payee are not known to each other. In many commercial transactions, the sellers of goods and services prefer to have a payment instrument where the sum of money payable to the payee is guaranteed. The demand draft is one such instrument.

Cheque volumes have risen steadily in all urban centres, their growth in metropolitan centres and other major cities being much faster than the rest. Mumbai, for example, has a substantially higher volume than the other metropolitan centres. In recent times, cheque volumes in cities such as Ahmedabad, Surat and Vadodara have registered sharp increases.

The growth of cheque volumes could be attributed partly to the rapid expansion of bank branches through the seventies and the consequent spread of banking as also partly to the increasing tendency of the people to invest in financial assets like shares and debentures. There has also been a significant growth in such corporate instruments as fixed deposits. This is reflected in the substantial increase in the use of payable *at par* instruments for dividends, interests and refund orders.

The substantial increase in the volumes of cheques indicates the need for upgrading the existing infrastructure for exchange and settlement from manual clearing arrangement to more efficient and electronically driven systems. Manual sorting and listing of instruments result in long delays as well as errors in computation of the total claims. The settlement process itself would get delayed and result in the problem of unreconciled entries between the banks.

2.2.2 Demand Draft: The demand draft is a pre-paid negotiable instrument, wherein the drawee bank undertakes to make payment in full when the instrument is presented by the payee for payment. The demand draft is made payable on a specified branch of a bank at a specified centre. In order to obtain payment, the beneficiary has to either present the instrument directly to the branch concerned or have it collected by his/her bank through the clearing mechanism.

2.2.3 Banker's Cheque: Banker's cheque is another payment instrument which is used by banks to settle payment obligations on behalf of their customers. This instrument is guaranteed by the bank for its full value and is similar to a demand draft. In practice, these instruments are payable at the branch of issue and are used for payment within the local clearing jurisdiction.

2.2.4 Payment Orders: Payment orders are issued by banks for payments made on behalf of the bank. These instruments are signed by a banker and carry the guarantee of the bank on the availability of the funds. These instruments are payable at the branch of issue.

2.2.5 Travellers Cheques: Carrying large amounts of cash is very risky, especially when one is travelling. Travellers' cheques are a secure and convenient alternative to carrying cash. These are pre-paid instruments available in fixed denominations. The holder of the travellers' cheque is required to sign the instrument upon purchase and again in the presence of the merchant establishment at the time of making payment or realising proceeds thereof. Travellers' cheques can be replaced if they are lost or stolen at no additional cost. Travellers' cheques are available in both domestic and international currency. These instruments can be readily exchanged at bank branches anywhere and in several merchant establishments.

2.2.6 Interest Warrant: The payment of periodic interest on fixed deposits with companies as well as government securities is a different class of payment for which a special type of payment instrument called an *interest warrant* is issued. These are special types of cheques which are *payable at par* in various branches of a bank across the country. The term *at par* indicates that the full face value of the instrument has to be credited to the account of the payee, without recourse to any deductions in the form of collection charges, which banks usually levy whenever an instrument is sent for collection. Dividend warrants too are similar to the interest warrants and are usually payable 'at par' to the shareholders of a company.

Interest warrants have been in vogue for a very long time, as can be recognised by the fact that servicing of public debt entails payment of interest to holders of Government securities. The servicing of public debt is done by the Public Debt Office of the Reserve Bank of India, which issues interest warrants, payable *at par* at all offices of Reserve Bank of India and State Bank of India.

2.2.7 Dividend Warrants: Interest or dividend warrants and refund orders are issued by the companies with a prior funding arrangement with a bank. The company funds an account with the bank with a sum equal to at least the total value of the interest warrants proposed to be issued. The bank, provides the *at par* facility whereby the instruments drawn on that particular bank are payable at par in selected branches of the bank as also the branches of the correspondent bank at various centres across the country. These warrants are honoured by the paying branches and the funding account of the company is debited.

Corporate clients are also extended the facility to issue current account cheques *at par* by their bankers on a very selective basis. This is largely done to facilitate payments to upcountry suppliers and others. Similarly for payments from retailers and other upcountry buyers of corporate products, banks offer collection accounts facilities to reputed companies. The payments to the company are channelled through special accounts throughout the country and repatriated to the headquarters' account.

The payment instruments described above are all paper-based and require to be tendered at specific banks for payment either in person or through another bank in clearing or through collection. Under the NI Act, 1881, the cheque or the instrument has to be presented to the drawer. The chief disadvantage with the cheque and the demand draft is that these instruments have to be physically presented, often leading to delays in payment. To overcome delays, fund transfers through the medium of telex were introduced. The telegraphic transfers represent payment instructions sent in a telex mode to an upcountry branch of the same bank or to a correspondent bank branch to credit the beneficiary's account with a given amount. A cipher code is appended to the text of the message to ensure its integrity and authenticity during transit.

2.2.8 Other Payment Instruments: Some other important payment instruments which became popular before the advent of electronic transfers were as under:

A. Money Order: Money order service is offered by the Department of Posts, Government of India. The money order enables an individual to send remittances to a third party under the aegis of the post office. It is a point-to-point delivery of funds. The originating post office collects the full amount of remittance as also a commission (service charge) from the individual remitting the funds and sends the advice to the destination post office. At the destination post office, the funds are paid to the beneficiary. The money order can be sent as an ordinary paper-based payment advice or as a *telegraphic money order*. The telegraphic money order is faster as the payment advices are sent through telex or telegraph. The customer, of course, has to pay higher service charges for this facility.

The postal order is another payment instrument of the Department of Posts. The postal order is issued denomination-wise, which can be encashed by the beneficiary after due identification at the post office on which it is drawn. Postal orders like the money orders are independent of the banking system.

2.3 Clearing Infrastructure

The membership of the clearing house includes both direct members and sub-members. All the branches of a member bank within the clearing house jurisdiction are eligible to present and receive cheques drawn on any other member bank/branch within the jurisdiction. The sub-members, who are sponsored by a member bank, participate in clearing in the same way as a branch of a member bank.

The dominant feature of the Indian banking system is its branch-cantered banking. The vast network of branches implies that the logistics of collection and delivery of paper payment instruments becomes formidable. The clearing infrastructure is designed to address the movement of instruments between the presenting and drawee branches. Each member bank in a centre is represented in the clearing house by its service branch which collects all the instruments from various branches and consolidates them for presentation to all the banks in the clearing house. Similarly, it receives and distributes among its branches all the instruments drawn upon its branches by other banks in the clearing house. The service branch of a bank performs a crucial intermediary role between the clearing house and the branch of a bank.

The clearing process begins with the deposit of a cheque in a bank. The cheque (along with other cheques) is delivered to the bank/branch where it is drawn. The cheque is passed for payment if the funds are available and the banker is satisfied about the genuineness of the instrument. The cheques that are unpaid are returned to the presenting bank through another clearing called the return clearing. The realisation of the funds occurs after the completion of return clearing and by the absence of an unpaid cheque.

The settlement of funds in clearing occurs at several levels. The aggregate amount or value of cheques presented by a bank on other banks represents the claim by that bank on other banks. Similar claims are made by all the banks on every other bank in the clearing. A net settlement is arrived at the clearing house and the debit or credit position of the bank is determined. These are booked in their current accounts maintained by the settling bank. This represents the inter-bank settlement. The settlement of funds between the service branch and the branch concerned represents the transfer of funds to the branch level. The payment process is completed only when the funds are debited from the drawer's account and credited to the payee's account. This occurs after the completion of the return clearing.

The total clearing cycle including the return clearing introduces a time lag in the payments process. The need for physical presentment of the cheque at the branch where it is drawn on, requires the movement of cheques from one place to another. As a result, the recipient of payment has to wait until the collecting banker is fully satisfied that the cheque has been paid. This time lag will continue irrespective of the level of technology and improvements in process, so long as the physical presentment of the cheque is necessary as per the banking law.

As the clearing jurisdiction is local, a separate procedure has evolved for the collection of cheques drawn on banks outside the clearing house area. In this case, the cheques are sent by post for collection to the representative branch or correspondent branch for presentation in the clearing house in the outstation centre. Once the cheque is realised, the proceeds are remitted to the original presenting bank for credit to the customer account. This leads to a significant delay in the payment of these cheques and there is considerable uncertainty regarding the time of realisation.

Prior to 1986, there were no formal regulations and rules governing the transaction of business in the clearing houses. Each Clearing House had its own rules and regulations based on local conventions and convenience. In case of disputes, problem resolution proved to be a tricky exercise.

In 1986, Reserve Bank of India framed a set of guidelines known as the Uniform Regulations and Rules (URR) for the Bankers' Clearing Houses. These guidelines were prescribed against the backdrop of considerable changes occurring in the functioning of the clearing houses due to the introduction of computerisation in the banking industry.

The Regulations are designed to provide a uniform framework for the conduct of clearing throughout the country and have been adopted individually by the general body of each clearing house in the country. Individual Clearing Houses are free to frame their own rules consistent with the broad framework provided by the Regulations.

URR represents a significant step forward in providing a formal institutional framework for the payments system in the country. They govern the conduct of the clearing business, prescribe a fair membership criteria and provide for penalties in the case of default. They also explicitly provide for significant oversight function for the Reserve Bank of India.

2.4 Computerisation of Clearing and Settlement Operations

Computerisation of clearing operations was the first major step towards modernisation of the payments system. The introduction of technology for clearing operations began with the setting up of Claim-based Settlement System using microprocessor based computer systems at Mumbai, Chennai and Delhi, in the early 1980s. These systems were used for generating settlement reports on the basis of input statements containing the aggregate value of (cheques presented) claims of one bank over the other banks in the clearing house. Clearing balancing and settlement, which used to take a long time due to differences and errors in manual balancing, were reduced, apart from providing accuracy in the final settlement.

The next important milestone was fully automating the clearing operations. The rapid growth of cheque volumes in the eighties made the task of manual sorting and listing a very difficult task. Banks were unable to cope with the huge volume of cheques which had to be physically handled prior to their presentation in the clearing house. Though the clearing settlement became easy because of computerisation, the heavy volumes of paper that had to be processed, introduced delays in presentation resulting in delayed credit to the customers. The growth in the volumes could therefore, be managed only by mechanisation of the entire clearing process.

The solution was the introduction of magnetic ink character recognition (MICR) based mechanised cheque processing technology. The existing cheques had to be redesigned incorporating a MICR codeline which could be read by document processing machines called reader-sorters.

The magnetic media based input settlement represents an intermediate step towards complete automation of cheque clearing through MICR processing and enables banks and the clearing house to get accustomed to a computerised environment. The system has been in operation for nearly four years and is functioning satisfactorily. It covers presentation clearing, return clearing, high value/high value return clearings and inter-bank clearing but does not cover inter-city clearing.

Computerisation of service branches which accompanied the computerisation of the clearing houses (both MICR and Floppy based) at banking centres with large volumes of business has resulted in the creation of a base for the introduction of automated clearing operations at other centres. This has also enabled the introduction of electronic payments services on an experimental basis so that future expansion of these services using the clearing infrastructure is possible. However, there is a lot of scope for developing backward and forward linkages to fully utilise the advantage of the item-wise database created by the MICR cheque processing.

2.5 Electronic Payment Systems

By the early 1990s, MICR computerised cheque clearing operations at the 4 metropolitan centres i.e. Mumbai, Calcutta, Chennai and New Delhi had stabilised. However, the volumes in cheque clearing continued to reflect an upward trend, creating considerable pressure on the existing work flow processes. A closer analysis revealed that at par' items such as dividend and interest warrants issued by various corporates were contributing significantly to the volumes in clearing. The existing system of paying interest/dividend to the beneficiaries through paper instruments is also fraud prone with frequent reports of postal interception and encashment, often resulting in the real beneficiaries not getting their dues at all, or at other times getting delayed payments.

It was decided that a system needed to be put in place that would: (a) decrease the volumes of paper instruments in MICR clearing and (b) improve customer service by ensuring prompt and secure interest/dividend payments to the beneficiaries. Such a system needed to be cost-effective and serve as an alternate method of effecting bulk, low value, recurring payment transactions, thereby obviating the need to issue and handle paper instruments. Electronic Clearing Service (ECS) Credit scheme provided the answer to these problems.

In ECS Credit, a series of electronic payment instructions are generated to replace paper instruments. The system works on the basis of one single debit transaction triggering a large number of credit entries. These credits or electronic payment instructions which possess details of the beneficiary's account number, amount and bank branch, are then communicated to the bank branches through their respective service branches for crediting the accounts of the beneficiaries either through magnetic media duly encrypted or through hard copy.

User institutions, usually corporate bodies/government departments which have to effect payments to large number of beneficiaries submit details of payments in magnetic media to the bank managing the clearing house, through a sponsor bank. The user institutions are required to obtain mandates from beneficiaries, for crediting their accounts under ECS. The corporate bodies too should on their own, advice the beneficiaries about the due date of credit under ECS.

2.6 Automated Teller Machines (ATMs)

Stand-alone ATMs made their appearance in India, in the early 1990s. These were mostly installed by foreign banks in their branch premises, as per the then existing policy. Easing of restrictions on the location of ATMs has led to their being installed at convenient places such as airports, central business districts, hospitals etc.

ATMs are primarily used for performing some of the banking functions such as withdrawal of cash or deposit of cash/cheque etc., by using an ATM card. Each customer is provided with an ATM card with a unique personal identification number (PIN). Whenever a customer performs a transaction, the person has to key in the PIN which is validated by the ATM, before the machine permits any transaction. The PIN has to be kept secret by the customer, to prevent any misuse or fraudulent transactions in the event of loss of the card.

3

Reserve Bank of India (RBI) and Payment Systems

Payment and settlement systems are at the heart of a modern economy. Recognising this, RBI has been, over the years, initiating measures that have resulted in the payment systems in India gaining international recognition. The recent past has witnessed significant developments in this area, which have brought in a sea-change in the way our citizens use technology-based systems and products to take care of their funds transfer requirements.

RBI's vision for the payment and settlement systems is to encourage greater use of electronic payments by all sections of society. This is aided by the establishment of a robust backbone to meet the economy's requirements, while ensuring safety, security and universal reach with technological solutions that hasten processing, as also improve the user-convenience dimension. While the RBI continues to pay focused attention to appropriate enabling regulation, strong infrastructure, apposite supervision and customer centricity, due attention must be paid by operators towards cyber security, effective customer grievance redress arrangements and reasonableness of customer charges. Operators should ensure that no corner is cut regarding cyber security.

Central banks worldwide are involved in payment and settlement systems in a number of ways. They provide settlement accounts, oversee core payment arrangements, and operate, provide and use various payment services.

In India, RBI regulates and supervises payment and settlement systems with the objective of promoting safety and efficiency by monitoring the existing and planned systems, assessing them against the stated objectives and, where necessary, inducing change. The oversight of payment and settlement systems has become more distinct and formal in recent years as part of a growing concern with financial stability as also with the increasing role of private participants in financial transactions. The increasing attention by the RBI also reflects the large increase in the value of transfers cleared and settled, the increasing centralisation of transactions around a small number of key systems and the growing technological complexity.

3.1 Payment System Initiatives of RBI

The central bank of any country is usually the driving force in the development of national payment systems. RBI as the central bank of India has been playing this developmental role and has taken several initiatives for safe, secure, sound, efficient, accessible and authorised payment systems in the country. The Board for Regulation and Supervision of Payment and Settlement Systems (BPSS), a sub-committee of the Central Board of the Reserve Bank of India is the highest policy making body on payment systems in the country. The BPSS is empowered for authorising, prescribing policies and setting standards for regulating and supervising all the payment and settlement systems in the country. The Department of Payment and Settlement Systems of the Reserve Bank of India serves as the Secretariat to the Board and executes its directions. In India, the payment and settlement systems are regulated by the Payment and Settlement Systems Act, 2007 (PSS Act) which was legislated in December 2007. [1]

The PSS Act as well as the Payment and Settlement System Regulations, 2008 framed thereunder came into effect from August 12, 2008. In terms of Section 4 of the PSS Act, no person other than the RBI can commence or operate a payment system in India unless authorised by the RBI. The RBI has since authorised payment system operators of pre-paid payment instruments, card schemes, cross-border in-bound money transfers, ATM networks and centralised clearing arrangements.

The RBI has taken many initiatives towards introducing and upgrading safe and efficient modes of payment systems in the country to meet the requirements of the public at large.

The dominant features of large geographic spread of the country and the vast network of branches of the Indian banking system require the logistics of collection and delivery of paper instruments. These aspects of the banking structure in the country have always been kept in mind while developing the payment systems.

At present, there are payments in India can be made through paper based instruments, electronic instruments and other instruments, such as, pre-paid systems, mobile banking, ATM based, point-of-sale terminals, online transactions.

3.1.1 Paper-based Payments: Use of paper-based clearing instruments (like cheques, drafts, and the like) accounted for nearly 7.4 percent of the volume of retail payments in the country at end-March 2018.

This share has been steadily decreasing over a period of time and electronic mode gained popularity due to the concerted efforts of the Reserve Bank of India to popularize the electronic payment products in preference to cash and cheques.

Since paper based payments occupy an important place in the country, RBI had introduced MICR technology for speeding up and bringing in efficiency in processing of cheques.

Later, a separate high value clearing was introduced for clearing cheques of value of ₹ 1 lakh and above. This clearing was available at select large centres in the country (since discontinued). Recent developments in paper-based instruments include launch of speed clearing (for local clearance of outstation cheques drawn on core-banking enabled branches of banks), introduction of cheque truncation (CTS) system (to restrict physical movement of cheques and enable use of images for payment processing), framing CTS-2010 Standards (for enhancing the security features on cheque forms) and the like.

While the overall thrust is to reduce the use of paper for transactions, given the fact that it would take some time to completely move to the electronic mode, the intention is to reduce the movement of paper—both for local and outstation clearance of cheques.

3.1.2 Electronic Payments: The initiatives taken by the RBI in the mid-eighties and early-nineties focused on technology-based solutions for the improvement of the payment and settlement system infrastructure, coupled with the introduction of new payment products by taking advantage of the technological advancements in banks. The continued increase in the volume of cheques added pressure on the existing set-up, thus necessitating a cost-effective alternative system.

A. Electronic Clearing Service (ECS) Credit:

- RBI introduced the ECS (Credit) Scheme during the 1990s to handle bulk and repetitive payment requirements (like salary, interest, dividend payments) of corporates and other institutions. ECS (Credit) facilitates customer accounts to be credited on the specified value date and is presently available at all major cities in the country.
- During September 2008, the Bank launched a new service known as National Electronic Clearing Service (NECS), at National Clearing Cell (NCC), Mumbai. NECS (Credit) facilitates multiple credits to beneficiary accounts with destination branches across the country against a single debit of the account of the sponsor bank. The system has a pan-India characteristic and leverages on core banking solutions (CBS) of member banks, facilitating all CBS bank branches to participate in the system, irrespective of their location across the country.

B. Regional ECS (RECS): Next to NECS, RECS has been launched during the year 2009. RECS, a miniature of the NECS, is confined to bank branches within the jurisdiction of a regional office of the RBI. Under the system, the sponsor bank will upload the validated data through the secured web server of RBI containing credit/debit instructions to the customers of CBS-enabled bank branches spread across the Jurisdiction of the Regional office of RBI. The RECS centre will process the data, arrive at the settlement, generate destination bank wise data/reports and make available the data/reports through secured web-server to facilitate the destination bank branches to afford credit/debit to the accounts of beneficiaries by leveraging the CBS technology put in place by the bank. Presently, RECS is available in 9 centres and locations across the country.

C. Electronic Clearing Service (ECS) Debit: The ECS (Debit) Scheme was introduced by RBI to provide a faster method of effecting periodic and repetitive collections of utility companies. ECS (Debit) facilitates consumers/ subscribers of utility companies to make routine and repetitive payments by 'mandating' bank branches to debit their accounts and pass on the money to the companies. This tremendously minimises use of paper instruments apart from improving process efficiency and customer satisfaction. There is no limit as to the minimum or maximum amount of payment. This is also available across major cities in the country.

D. Electronic Funds Transfer (EFT): This retail funds transfer system introduced in the late 1990s enabled an account holder of a bank to electronically transfer funds to another account holder with any other participating bank. Available across 15 major centres in the country, this system is no longer available for use by the general public, for whose benefit a feature-rich and more efficient system is now in place, which is the NEFT system.

E. National Electronic Funds Transfer (NEFT) System: In November 2005, a more secure system was introduced for facilitating one-to-one funds transfer requirements of individuals/corporates. Available across a longer time window, the NEFT system provides for batch settlements at hourly intervals, thus enabling near real-time transfer of funds.

Certain other unique features viz. accepting cash for originating transactions, initiating transfer requests without any minimum or maximum amount limitations, facilitating one-way transfers to Nepal, receiving confirmation of the date/time of credit to the account of the beneficiaries, etc., are available in the system.

F. Real Time Gross Settlement (RTGS) System: RTGS is a funds transfer systems where transfer of money takes place from one bank to another on a "real time" and on "gross" basis. Settlement in "real time" means payment transaction is not subjected to any waiting period. "Gross settlement" means the transaction is settled on one to one basis without bunching or netting with any other transaction. Once processed, payments are final and irrevocable. This was introduced in 2004 and settles all inter-bank payments and customer transactions above ₹ 2 lakh.

G. Clearing Corporation of India Limited (CCIL): CCIL was set up in April 2001 by banks, financial institutions and primary dealers, to function as an industry service organisation for clearing and settlement of trades in money market, government securities and foreign exchange markets.

The Clearing Corporation plays the crucial role of a central counter party (CCP) in the government securities, USD-INR forex exchange (both spot and forward segments) and collaterised borrowing and lending obligation (CBLO) markets. CCIL plays the role of a central counterparty whereby, the contract between buyer and seller gets replaced by two new contracts between CCIL and each of the two parties. This process is known as 'Novation'. Through novation, the counterparty credit risk between the buyer and seller is eliminated with CCIL subsuming all counterparty and credit risks. In order to minimize the risks, that it exposes itself to, CCIL follows specific risk management practices which are as per international best practices.

In addition to the guaranteed settlement, CCIL also provides non-guaranteed settlement services for National Financial Switch (Inter-bank ATM transactions) and for rupee derivatives such as interest rate swaps.

CCIL is also providing a reporting platform and acts as a repository for over the counter (OTC) products.

3.1.3 Other Payment Systems: These are as under:

A. Pre-paid Payment Systems: Pre-paid instruments are payment instruments that facilitate purchase of goods and services against the value stored on these instruments. The value stored on such instruments represents the value paid for by the holders by cash, by debit to a bank account, or by credit card. The pre-paid payment instruments can be issued in the form of smart cards, magnetic stripe cards, internet accounts, internet wallets, mobile accounts, mobile wallets, paper vouchers etc.

Subsequent to the notification of the PSS Act, policy guidelines for issuance and operation of prepaid instruments in India were issued in the public interest to regulate the issue of prepaid payment instruments in the country.

The use of pre-paid payment instruments for cross border transactions has not been permitted, except for the payment instruments approved under Foreign Exchange Management Act,1999 (FEMA).

B. Mobile Banking System: Mobile phones as a medium for providing banking services have been attaining increased importance. Reserve Bank brought out a set of operating guidelines on mobile banking for banks in October 2008, according to which only banks which are licensed and supervised in India and have a physical presence in India are permitted to offer mobile banking after obtaining necessary permission from RBI. The guidelines focus on systems for security and inter-bank transfer arrangements through RBI's authorized systems. On the technology front the objective is to enable the development of inter-operable standards so as to facilitate funds transfer from one account to any other account in the same or any other bank on a real time basis irrespective of the mobile network a customer has subscribed to.

C. ATMs, Point-of-Sale (POS) Terminals, and Online Transactions: As on April 30, 2019, there were 2,07,131 ATMs in India. Savings bank customers can withdraw cash from any bank terminal up to 5 times in a month without being charged for the same. To address the customer service issues arising out of failed ATM transactions where the customer's account gets debited without actual disbursal of cash, the RBI has mandated re-crediting of such failed transactions within 7 working days and mandated compensation for delays beyond the stipulated period. Furthermore, a standardised template has been prescribed for displaying at all ATM locations to facilitate lodging of complaints by customers.

There were 37,57,621 PoS terminals in the country at end-April 2019, which enable customers to make payments for purchases of goods and services by means of credit/debit cards. To facilitate customer convenience the RBI has also permitted cash withdrawal using debit cards issued by the banks at PoS terminals.

The PoS for accepting card payments also include online payment gateways. This facility is used for enabling online payments for goods and services. The online payment are enabled through own payment gateways or third party service providers called intermediaries.

In payment transactions involving intermediaries, these intermediaries act as the initial recipient of payments and distribute the payment to merchants.

In such transactions, the customers are exposed to the uncertainty of payment as most merchants treat the payments as final on receipt from the intermediaries. In this regard safeguard the interests of customers and to ensure that the payments made by them using electronic/online payment modes are duly accounted for by intermediaries receiving such payments, directions were issued in November 2009.

Directions require that the funds received from customers for such transactions need to be maintained in an internal account of a bank and the intermediary should not have access to the same.

Further, to reduce the risks arising out of the use of credit/debit cards over internet/IVR [technically referred to as card not present (CNP) transactions], RBI mandated that all CNP transactions should be additionally authenticated based on information not available on the card and an online alert should be sent to the cardholders for such transactions.

3.1.4 Oversight of Payment and Settlement Systems: Oversight of the payment and settlement systems is a central bank function whereby the objectives of safety and efficiency are promoted by monitoring existing and planned systems, assessing them against these objectives and, where necessary, inducing change. By overseeing payment and settlement systems, central banks help to maintain systemic stability and reduce systemic risk, and to maintain public confidence in payment and settlement systems. The Payment and Settlement Systems Act, 2007, and the Payment and Settlement Systems Regulations, 2008, framed there under, provide the necessary statutory backing to the Reserve Bank of India for undertaking the oversight function over the payment and settlement systems in the country.

3.2 Board for Regulation and Supervision of Payment and Settlement Systems (BPSS)

In order to provide focused attention to the payment and settlement systems, the RBI constituted the BPSS as a Committee of its Central Board. The Reserve Bank of India (Board for Regulation and Supervision of Payment and Settlement Systems) Regulations, 2005 was notified in the Gazette of India on February 18, 2005. The BPSS is headed by the Governor of the RBI with the Deputy Governor in-charge of payment and settlement systems as the Vice-Chairman and the other Deputy Governors and two members of the Central Board of the RBI as members. Functions and powers of the BPSS include the following.

1. Formulating policies relating to the regulation and supervision of all types of payment and settlement systems.
2. Setting standards for existing and future systems.
3. Authorising the payment and settlement systems.

4. Determining criteria for membership.

The National Payments Council, which was set up in 1999, has been designated as a Technical Advisory Committee of the BPSS. To assist the BPSS in performing its functions, a new department, the Department of Payments and Settlement Systems (DPSS), was set up in the RBI in March 2005.

The Board at its meetings had emphasised, *inter alia*, the following.

1. Payment system services in India should be taken to a level comparable with the best in the world.
2. Appropriate legal infrastructure may be created as early as possible.
3. A plan be drawn up to "leapfrog" from cash to electronic modes of payment, wherever possible.
4. Cheque clearing system would have to be made more efficient through cheque truncation system.
5. Usage of the RTGS system be increased both in terms of opening additional branch outlets and more number of transactions being put through.

3.3 RBI's Vision Documents for Payments

3.3.1 Vision Document for Payment Systems, 2005-08: In the recent period, the RBI has taken a number of initiatives to strengthen the institutional, technological and procedural framework for the payment and settlement systems. To carry forward these initiatives in an integrated and cohesive manner, a Vision Document for 2005-08 was prepared after taking into consideration the feedback from the various stakeholders such as banks, technology solution providers, members of public and other experts in the field. The Vision Document set out the roadmap for implementing the vision for payment and settlement systems within the next three years. The key themes of the action plans identified in the Vision Document were safety, security, soundness and efficiency (Triple-S and E). While safety in payment and settlement systems related to risk reduction measures, security implied confidence in the integrity of the payment systems. All payment systems were envisaged to be on a sound footing with adequate legal backing for operational procedures and transparency norms. Efficiency enhancements were envisaged by leveraging the benefits of technology for cost effective solutions.

The main action points for Payment and Settlement Systems, 2005-08 as set out in the Vision Document are indicated below:

A. Action Points during 2005-06:

1. Pursuing with Indian Banks' Association and major banks for setting up of a national level entity which will operate all retail payment systems in the country.
2. Operationalising National Settlement System for all clearings at four metro centres by December 2005.
3. Finalising the proposed EFT regulations.
4. Implementing Stage-2 of RTGS System, i.e., integrated accounting system (IAS)-RTGS rollout during which all inter-bank transactions at all major centres would be settled on RTGS platform and paper-based inter-bank clearing will be closed.
5. Pursuing with RTGS participants to cover all their networked branches under RTGS framework paving way for RTGS-based customer related transactions at about ten thousand branches in the country.
6. Implementing image-based CTS in the National Capital Region (NCR) on a pilot basis.
7. Preparing minimum standard of operational efficiency at MICR cheque processing centre (CPC).
8. Making available EFT facility at 500 capital market intensive centres as identified by BSE and NSE.
9. Setting up customer facilitation centre (CFC) at the RBI for various segments of national payment systems.
10. Public disclosure from each payment service provider of its standards, terms and conditions under which the payment will be effected and also compensation policy and procedure for any deficiency in services including the

setting up of CFC.

11. Drafting the Red Book on payment systems in India.
12. Drafting a comprehensive legislation on payment system.

B. Action Points during 2006-07:

1. To complete the tasks initiated during 2005-06.
2. To extend MICR clearing to 20 additional identified centres.
3. To ensure that every cheque issued follows MICR format and standards.
4. To implement EFT systems at a national level through the new retail payment institution.
5. To take all payment systems in India compliant with the core principles for systemically important payment systems (SIPS).
6. To increase the reach of payment services by means of tie-up and collaboration with other large coverage entities such as the post offices.
7. To facilitate government payments and receipts through electronic mode.

C. Action Points during 2007-08:

1. Creating off-city back-up arrangements for large value national payment systems such as RTGS and G-Sec clearing.
2. Making fully functional the new organisation for retail payment systems with all such payment under its umbrella.
3. Regulating various payment systems.
4. Ensuring cheque truncation based clearing at Mumbai, Chennai and Kolkata.
5. Covering National Settlement System at all major clearing houses/clearing organisations in the country.

3.3.2 Vision Document for Payment Systems, 2012-15: The main focus of the Vision Document for Payments Systems, 2012-15 was to provide a thrust to modern electronic payments that are safe, simple and low-cost for use by all. The document aimed at increasing the share of electronic payment transactions and taking measures towards moving to a less cash society and customer convenience.

The focus of cheque clearing operations in the coming years would be consolidation, rationalisation, centralisation, through the implementation of grid-based CTS solution (which is Information Technology Act compliant) across the country by NPCI. The grid-based CTS will usher in a standardised cheque clearing scenario across the country. The issuance of CTS 2010 compliant cheques will facilitate this process. Introduction of user/customer friendly features and increasing the number of settlement cycles in NEFT would be further examined.

3.3.3 Payment and Settlement Systems in India: Vision 2018: The *Vision 2018 for Payment and Settlement Systems in India* reiterates the commitment of the RBI to encourage greater use of electronic payments by all sections of society so as to achieve a *less-cash* society. The objective is to facilitate provision of a payment system for the future that combines the much-valued attributes of safety, security and universal reach with technological solutions which enable faster processing, enhanced convenience, and the extraction and use of valuable information that accompanies payments.

A. Vision Statement: Building best of class payment and settlement systems for a *less-cash* India through responsive regulation, robust infrastructure, effective supervision and customer centricity.

The broad contours of Vision 2018 revolve around the 5Cs:

1. Coverage—by enabling wider access to a variety of electronic payment services.
2. Convenience—by enhancing user experience through ease of use and of products and processes.
3. Confidence—by promoting integrity of systems, security of operations and customer protection.
4. Convergence—by ensuring interoperability across service providers.
5. Cost—by making services cost effective for users as well as service providers.

Vision 2018 focuses on four strategic initiatives viz.,

responsive regulation, robust infrastructure, effective supervision and customer centricity.

Firstly, RBI, in consultation with all the stakeholders, will continue its efforts to create a regulatory framework to promote twin objectives of enhanced coverage with interoperability of the payments system and convenience with security for the end-users in sync with emerging developments and innovations.

Secondly, building a robust payments infrastructure in the country to increase the accessibility, availability, interoperability and security of the payment systems will continue to remain a key objective.

Thirdly, Vision 2018 will focus on effectiveness of supervisory mechanisms to strengthen the resilience of the financial market infrastructures (FMIs) and system wide important payment systems (SWIPS) in the country besides setting up appropriate oversight framework for new systems, and augmenting the data reporting and fraud monitoring systems.

Finally, Vision 2018 will adopt a customer-centric approach to streamline the customer grievance redressal mechanism, focus on building customer awareness and education, and initiate customer protection measures.

B. Expected Outcomes of Vision 2018: New policies that are proposed to be framed under Vision 2018 with focus on electronic payments will influence the trends in payment systems in the country. Taking into account the positive developments during the period under Vision 2012-2015, and with the concerted efforts of the Government and all other stakeholders like banks, payment system operators, users, etc., Vision 2018 is expected to result in:

1. Continued decrease in the share of paper-based clearing instruments;
2. Consistent growth in individual segments of retail electronic payment systems viz. NEFT, IMPS, card transactions, mobile banking, etc.;
3. Increase in registered customer base for mobile banking;
4. Significant growth in acceptance infrastructure; and

5. Accelerated use of Aadhaar in payment systems.

3.3.4 Payment and Settlement Systems in India: Vision 2019-21: RBI's Vision Document on Payment and Settlement Systems, released on May 15, 2019, has the core theme of Empowering Exceptional (E) Payment Experience.

Vision 2021 concentrates on a two-pronged approach of, (a) exceptional customer experience; and (b) enabling an eco-system which will result in this customer experience. With this in view, the Vision aims towards,

1. Enhancing the experience of customers.
2. Empowering payment system operators and service providers.
3. Enabling the eco-system and infrastructure.
4. Putting in place a forward-looking regulation.
5. Supported by a risk-focussed supervision.

To achieve the above, the Vision envisages four goal-posts (4 Cs): Competition, Cost, Convenience and Confidence.

To sum up, several steps have been taken by the RBI in recent years to improve customer service of commercial banks. In the context of the rapidly evolving financial landscape, RBI has also been suitably reorienting its regulatory and supervisory framework to meet the needs of the common man. It has also been the endeavour of RBI to improve credit delivery and customer service by banks. RBI has simultaneously focussed on financial inclusion and extension of banking services to the unbanked areas of the economy. RBI has taken a host of measures in recent years aimed at providing customer service at reasonable cost. These measures include enhancing customer protection and disclosures, code of ethics and grievance redressal, among others. RBI's broad approach to financial inclusion aims at *connecting people* with the banking system and not just credit dispensation; giving people access to the payments system; and portraying financial inclusion as a viable business model and opportunity. RBI has been initiating measures to improve the outreach of banks and their services, and promote financial inclusion in less developed states and union territories.

A smooth and efficient payment and settlement infrastructure plays an important role in maintaining stability in the financial sector. Significant progress has been made in improving the payment systems infrastructure in India with the introduction of RTGS, operation of high value cheque clearing system (HVCCS), setting up of Clearing Corporation of India Limited (CCIL) as the central counterparty in the government securities, foreign exchange and collateralised borrowing and lending obligation (CBLO) segments as also setting up central counterparties (CCPs) for the settlement of equities and derivatives. The legal framework for payment and settlement systems has also been strengthened by the recent notification of the Payment and Settlement Systems Act and Rules. This has made India largely compliant with international standards and codes in this area.

Though there have been improvements in legal infrastructure in the financial sector like setting up of debt recovery tribunals (DRTs) and the enactment of the Securitisation and Reconstruction of Financial Assets and Enforcement of Security Interests (SARFAESI) Act, the major concern is that despite the robust insolvency laws the time taken for completion of liquidation proceedings is one of the highest in the world and the recovery rate one of the lowest.

Endnote

1. The PSS Act, 2007 received the assent of the President on December 20, 2007 and it came into force with effect from August 12, 2008. The PSS Act, 2007 provides for the regulation and supervision of payment systems in India and designates the Reserve Bank of India (Reserve Bank) as the authority for that purpose and all related matters. The Reserve Bank is authorized under the Act to constitute a Committee of its Central Board known as the Board for Regulation and Supervision of Payment and Settlement Systems (BPSS), to exercise its powers and perform its functions and discharge its duties under this statute.

4

Some Other Organizations Linked to Payment Systems

The area of clearing and settlement has witnessed substantial progress in Indian securities market over the last decade as a result of the various reforms initiated by the regulatory authorities.

4.1 Board for Regulation and Supervision of Payment and Settlement Systems (BPSS)

See section 3.2 of chapter 3 of this book.

4.2 Clearing Corporation of India Limited (CCIL)

CCIL was incorporated on April 30, 2001, to provide clearing and settlement services in government securities, foreign exchange and money market instruments. The RBI took the initiative of setting up the CCIL with State Bank of India (SBI), Industrial Development Bank of India (IDBI), Life Insurance Corporation of India (LIC), ICICI Bank Ltd., Bank of Baroda and HDFC Bank Ltd. as its core promoters. This initiative was taken recognising the need for upgrading the country's financial infrastructure in respect of clearing and settlement of debt instruments and forex transactions. CCIL currently provides guaranteed settlement facility for government securities clearing, clearing of collateralised borrowing and lending obligations (CBLO) and foreign exchange clearing.

CCIL-operated systems include the following:

4.2.1 Government Securities Segment: During 1996-2002, a quasi-DvP system was in place with the book-entry system in government securities not directly linked with the funds accounts, with no mechanism to prevent a gridlock in the system. In 2002, CCIL was constituted by the banks to play the role of a CCP and for providing a settlement guarantee mechanism. The government securities settlement system has evolved since then and transactions are now settled on a net basis. Settlement through CCIL has the following advantages: (a) assurance of settlement to the members on the settlement date, (b) reduction in counterparty exposure, (c) operational efficiency, and (d) improved liquidity.

CCIL provides guaranteed settlement of all secondary market outright sales and repo transactions in government securities by the process of novation. All trades reported on the RBI's NDS platform or contracted on the online anonymous, trading platform NDSOM, are accepted by CCIL for settlement after the necessary validations. These trades are settled on a DvP-III basis, i.e. the funds leg and the securities leg are settled on a net basis.

4.2.2 CBLO Segment: The CBLO is a money market product developed by CCIL and launched on January 20, 2003. The product was initially developed with a view to providing entities that have been phased out from the unsecured inter-bank call money market with an avenue for their funds operations. A repo variant, CBLO enables borrowing/lending of funds of various maturities up to one year, fully backed by collaterals in the form of central government securities/treasury bills. CCIL provides guaranteed settlement facility for trades in this instrument as a central counterparty. The funds leg of the trades in this instrument is settled in the current account maintained by these entities with the RBI. The borrowing and lending takes place through an electronic anonymous order matching platform. CBLO operates in a straight-through processing (STP)-enabled environment, seamlessly encompassing dealing to settlement.

The CBLO market has now become the preferred option for participants in the money market. The volume in this market is now significantly higher than the combined volumes in the call and the repo market.

4.2.3 Forex Segment: CCIL provides a guaranteed settlement facility for all US dollar-Indian Rupee inter-bank cash, tom, spot and forward transactions. The matched and accepted forward deals are guaranteed for settlement from S-2 day (two days previous to settlement) and the spot, tom, cash deals are guaranteed for settlement from the trade date as the CCIL becomes the central counterparty to every accepted trade through the process of novation. The rupee-leg of the transaction is settled through the member's current account with the RBI and the US dollar leg through CCIL's account with the Settlement Bank at New York.

CCIL also provides continuous-linked settlement (CLS) settlement services for banks in India by availing of third party services of a settlement bank. Banks participating in this segment of CCIL report their cross-currency trades to the settlement bank directly or through CCIL. The settlement is made through the nostro accounts of CCIL with the settlement bank in CLS settlement currencies.

The settlement of forex transactions by CCIL has resulted in a reduction in counterparty exposure, increased operational efficiency and overall lower operational costs. Forex settlement volumes in CCIL have been rising consistently through the years and have witnessed substantial growth since it commenced operations.

4.3 National Securities Clearing Corporation Ltd (NSCCL)

NSCCL, a wholly-owned subsidiary of NSE, was incorporated in August 1995 and commenced operating as a clearing corporation in April 1996. Clearing and settlement operations of the NSE are managed by NSCCL. It was the first clearing corporation to provide novation/settlement guarantee that revolutionised the entire concept of settlement system in India. It was set up to: (a) bring and sustain confidence in clearing and settlement of securities, (b) promote and maintain short and consistent settlement cycles, (c) provide counterparty risk guarantee, and (d) operate a tight risk containment system.

The settlements of trade in the equities market (both cash and derivative segments) are settled in the BSE by clearing house called BOISL which is a company, jointly promoted by BSE (49 percent) and Bank of India (51 percent). BOISL, *inter alia*, handles some of the settlement-related activities of BSE as per instructions and directions of BSE. Responsibility of the clearing house is to handle such settlement activities including co-ordination with the market participants, viz. depositories, clearing banks etc.

However, the overall responsibility of settlement and risk management functions, viz. collection of margins, collateral management etc. pertaining to transactions done on BSE Online Trading (BOLT) System lies with the BSE.

NSCCL undertakes clearing of transactions executed on the National Stock Exchange for Automated Trading (NEAT) system of NSE. It carries out clearing and settlement functions as per the settlement cycles of different sub-segments in the equities segment. The reforms in the securities settlement systems have resulted in following benefits:

1. Reduction and mitigation of systemic, structural and operational risks.
2. Increase speed of transaction, execution and settlement of trade and quicker settlement of transactions with finality.
3. Safety of the settlement process.
4. Reduction of transaction costs and, thereby, making market more efficient and transparent for investors and participants.

4.4 Government Securities Settlement System

The infrastructure for the government securities settlement systems in India is provided by the RBI. The Public Debt Office (PDO) in the RBI functions as the depository. The PDO has well-laid-down guidelines for opening subsidiary general ledger accounts (SGL) for recording all purchase and sales transactions in government securities. Secondary market transactions in government securities are settled in the books of the RBI for both securities leg and funds leg on delivery versus payment (DvP) basis.

A series of measures taken by the RBI has changed the

way the government securities settle currently in India:

- **July 1995: Introduction of Delivery versus Payment (DvP):** The system was DvP I, wherein securities and funds were settled on a gross basis. Through this, settlement risk has been greatly reduced.
- **February 2002: Establishment of Clearing Corporation of India (CCIL):** Acting as a central counterparty through novation, the CCIL provides guaranteed settlement and has put in place risk management systems to limit settlement risk and operates a settlement guarantee fund backed by lines of credit from commercial banks. The netting of funds by CCIL reduces the liquidity requirements of the market and thereby liquidity risk of the system. All the transactions in government securities market, concluded or reported on NDS and NDS-OM have to be necessarily settled through the CCIL.
- **February 2002: Introduction of Negotiated Dealing System (NDS):** Besides enabling electronic dealing and transparency in the system, the NDS-enabled paperless settlement of transactions in government securities with electronic connectivity to CCIL and the DvP settlement system at the Public Debt Office through electronic SGL transfer form. All entities having SGL Accounts with the RBI were advised to join the NDS-CCIL system by March 31, 2003.
- **May 2002: Introduction of Compulsory Holding of Government Securities in Demat Form:** Compulsory holding of government securities in demat form for the RBI-regulated entities was introduced to prevent possibility of fraudulent transactions in government securities held in physical form. This improved the efficiency of security settlements by reducing the time taken and aided in simplification of settlement procedures.
- **March 2004: Introduction of Real Time Gross Settlement System (RTGS):** Introduction of RTGS system was an important measure in improving the stability of settlements in

all inter-bank transactions including the government securities. The netted settlement files are also currently being submitted on RTGS for settlement. The system has integrated module for IDL against government securities. Towards the end of 2006, the total solution release (TSR) of RTGS has been implemented in which the security settlement system (SSS) has been integrated facilitating *on-demand* IDL facility for the market participants.

- **May 2005: Introduction of Standardised Settlement Cycle of T+1:** The settlement cycle for all outright OTC and NDS-OM trades in government securities was standardised to T+1 cycle for better fund management and risk management by the participants.

4.5 Committee to Review the Framework Related to Digital Payments

Ministry of Finance, Government of India had constituted this Committee on Digital Payments to review the payment systems in the country and to recommend appropriate measures for encouraging digital payments. The Committee (Chairman: Ratan P. Watal) was constituted on August 23, 2016 with the following terms of reference:

1. To study and recommend need for charges, if any, in the regulatory mechanism and any legislation, relevant for the purpose of promotion of payments by digital modes.
2. To study and recommend ways for leveraging Unique Identification Number or any other proof of identity for authentication of card/digital transactions and setting up of a Centralised KYC Registry.
3. To study introduction of single window system of Payment Gateway to accept all types of cards/digital payments of Government receipts.
4. To study feasibility and framing rules for creating a payments history of all digital payments and create necessary linkages between payments transaction history and credit information.

5. To study and recommend various measures to incentivize transactions through cards and digital means.
6. To study global best practices in payments including initiatives taken by various Governments/Government agencies.
7. To identify market failure(s), if any, along with suitable interventions that may be implemented to promote payment by card/digital means.
8. To identify regulatory bottlenecks, if any, and suggest changes to promote payment by card/digital means.
9. To study and make recommendations on any other matter related to promotion of payments through cards and digital means.

The Committee submitted an Interim Report to the Ministry of Finance on November 21, 2016. Towards finalization of the report, the Committee engaged extensively with all stakeholders and technology groups including the RBI, State Governments, Comptroller and Auditor General of India, payment companies, technology companies and the academia. The Committee submitted its Final Report to the Finance Minister on December 9, 2016.

The Committee, *inter alia*, recommended a medium-term strategy for accelerating growth of digital payments in India with a regulatory regime which is conducive to bridging the *digital divide* by promoting competition, open access and inter-operability in payments. The Committee recommended inclusion of financially and socially excluded groups and assimilation of emerging technologies in the market, while safeguarding security of digital transactions and providing level playing to all stakeholders and new players who will enter this new transaction space. It suggested inter-operability of the payments system between banks and non-banks, upgradation of the digital payment infrastructure and institutions and a framework to reward innovations and for leading efforts in enabling digital payments.

The Committee was seized of the developments following the decision of the Government to cancel legal tender character of currency of high denominations. The Committee calibrated its recommendations accordingly and provided a suitable framework for smooth and speedy transition towards a digital payments economy.

5

National Payments Corporation of India (NPCI): Products and Retail Payment Services

5.1 About NPCI

NPCI is an umbrella organization for all retail payments system in India. It was set up with the guidance and support of the RBI and Indian Banks' Association (IBA).

The RBI, after setting up the Board for Regulation and Supervision of Payment and Settlement Systems (BPSS) in 2005, released a vision document incorporating a proposal to set up an umbrella institution for all the retail payment systems in the country. The core objective was to consolidate and integrate the multiple systems with varying service levels into nation-wide uniform and standard business process for all retail payment systems. The other objective was to facilitate an affordable payment mechanism to benefit the common man across the country and help financial inclusion.

IBA's untiring efforts helped to turn this vision into a reality. NPCI was incorporated in December 2008 and the Certificate of Commencement of Business was issued in April 2009. It was incorporated as a Section 25 company under the Companies Act, 1956 (now Section 8 of Companies Act, 2013) and is aimed to operate for the benefit of all the member banks and their customers. The aim is to create infrastructure of large dimension and operate on high volumes resulting in payment services at a fraction of the present cost structure.

NPCI has ten promoter banks, namely State Bank of India, Punjab National Bank, Canara Bank, Bank of Baroda, Union Bank of India, Bank of India, ICICI Bank, HDFC Bank, Citibank and HSBC.

From a single service of switching of inter-bank ATM

transactions, the range of services has grown to cheque clearing, immediate payments service (24x7x365), automated clearing house, electronic benefit transfer and a domestic card payment network named RuPay to provide an alternative to international card schemes.

BPSS at its meeting held on September 24, 2009 had given an in-principle approval to issue authorization to NPCI for operating various retail payment systems in the country and granted certificate of authorization for operation of National Financial Switch (NFS) ATM Network with effect from October 15, 2009. NPCI had deputed its officials to IDRBT Hyderabad and had taken over NFS operations on December 14, 2009. Membership regulations and rules had been framed for enrolling all banks in the country as members. This was done so that when the nation-wide payment systems are launched, all would get included on a standardized platform.

One of the more successful products of NPCI has been the unified payments interface (UPI) that powers multiple bank accounts into a single mobile application (of any participating bank) for immediate fund transfers and a variety of payments without parting with sensitive information. It supports merchant payments, utility bill payments, "over-the-counter" payments, QR code (scan and pay)-based payments and the like, through mobile devices on a 365x24x7 basis. The UPI has exhibited significant growth since inception—both in volume and value terms—and has established itself as a veritable conduit for retail funds transfers.

The NPCI symbol uses the acronym of the organization's name. The letter forms are arranged to reflect solidity with progressiveness and dynamism. The use of the red dot and swirl make the entire image unique and memorable. The swirl also communicates worldwide presence. The green and red combination is reminiscent of the Indian National colours. It presents a fresh, individualistic and environmentally conscious message to the world.

The proximate objective behind NPCI is provision of

convenient *anytime-anywhere* payment services that are secure and easy-to-use. An attendant goal is to facilitate an affordable payment mechanism to benefit the common person and to catalyse financial inclusion as well. In a span of about a decade of its existence, NPCI has gained the status of being a systemically important payment infrastructure (SIPI).

India has been enjoying a very healthy evolution of payment systems. This has been the result of the calibrated approach adopted by the RBI—in the initial years as a developer, and in later years as a catalyst and facilitator. Today, India's systems are not only comparable to systems anywhere in the world, but they also set standards and good practices for others to emulate.

Products and services offered by NPCI are as under.

5.2 National Financial Switch (NFS)

The Institute of Development and Research in Banking Technology (IDRBT), Hyderabad had been providing ATM switching service to banks in India through National Financial Switch. IDRBT decided to hive off its operational role on ATM switching to have focus on research and development and was looking for a suitable arrangement for shifting this business to some national level payment system organization. National Payments Corporation of India (NPCI) considered this as an opportunity and started discussions with IDRBT on the feasibility of taking over.

The Board for Regulation and Supervision of Payment and Settlement systems (BPSS) at its meeting held on September 24, 2009 approved in-principle to issue authorisation to NPCI for operating various retail payment systems in the country. Reserve Bank of India also issued authorisation to NPCI to take over the operations of National Financial Switch (NFS) from the Institute of Development and Research in Banking Technology (IDRBT) on 'as is where is basis' on October 15, 2009. NPCI took over NFS operations from December 14, 2009.

The primary site for NFS is located at Mumbai and DR

site is located at Chennai.

5.3 Immediate Payment Services (IMPS)

5.3.1 Background: Currently, a majority of inter-bank mobile fund transfer transactions are channelised through NEFT mechanism. Under NEFT, the transactions are processed and settled in batches, hence are not real time. Also, the transactions can be done only during the working hours of the RTGS system.

In the above context, NPCI has carried out a pilot on mobile payment system initially with 4 member banks, viz. State Bank of India, Bank of India, Union Bank of India and ICICI Bank in August 2010. Yes Bank, Axis Bank and HDFC Bank have joined this pilot in month of September, October and November 2010 respectively. IMPS public launch happened on November 22, 2010 by Shrimati Shyamala Gopinath, DG RBI at Mumbai and this service is now available to the Indian public. As on June 20, 2019, 498 entities were live members of IMPS which includes small finance banks, public sector banks, private banks, payment banks, RRBs, co-operative banks and PPIs.

IMPS offers an instant, 24x7, inter-bank electronic fund transfer service through mobile phones. IMPS facilitates customers to use mobile instruments as a channel for accessing their bank accounts and put high inter-bank fund transfers in a secured manner with immediate confirmation features. This facility is provided by NPCI through its existing NFS switch.

The eligible criteria for the banks who can participate in IMPS is that the bank should have approval from RBI for mobile banking service.

A. Objectives of IMPS:

1. To enable bank customers to use mobile instruments as a channel for accessing their banks accounts and remit funds.
2. Making payment simpler just with the mobile number of the beneficiary.
3. To sub-serve the goal of RBI in electronification of retail payments.

4. To facilitate mobile payment systems already introduced in India with the Reserve Bank of India Mobile Payment Guidelines, 2008, to be inter-operable across banks and mobile operators in a safe and secured manner.
5. To build the foundation for a full range of mobile-based banking services.

B. Participants:

1. Remitter (Sender).
2. Beneficiary (Receiver).
3. Banks.
4. National Financial Switch-NPCI.

C. Pre-requisites for Mobile Banking through IMPS

(a) Registration for Remitter:

1. Register yourself for mobile banking service with bank.
2. Get mobile money identifier (MMID) and MPIN from the bank.
3. Download software (application) for mobile banking (ensure the compatibility of mobile with the application) or use the SMS facility in your mobile if your bank provides IMPS on SMS.

(b) Registration for Beneficiary:

1. Link your mobile number to the account in the respective bank.
2. Get mobile money identifier (MMID) from the bank.

(c) For Remitter (To send money):

1. Login to the application and select the IMPS menu from the IMPS or use the SMS facility in your mobile if your bank provides IMPS on SMS.
2. Get beneficiary mobile number and MMID.
3. Enter beneficiary mobile number, beneficiary MMID, amount and your MPIN to send.
4. Await confirmation SMS for the debit in your account and credit in beneficiary account.
5. Note the transaction reference number for any future query.
6. Share your mobile number and MMID with the remitter.
7. Ask the remitter to send money using your mobile number

and MMID.

8. Check the confirmation SMS for credit to your account from the remitter.
9. Note the transaction reference number for any future query.

5.3.2 Products: These are as under:

A. IMPS Funds Transfer from Person-to-Person (P2P): IMPS funds transfer offers an instant, 24x7, inter-bank electronic fund transfer service from one account to another account through mobile phones. IMPS funds transfer facilitate customers to use mobile instruments as a channel for accessing their bank accounts and put high inter-bank fund transfers in a secured manner with immediate confirmation features.

The key features of IMPS funds transfer are as follows:

1. Instant funds transfer.
2. 24x7x365 availability.
3. Credit and debit confirmations to sender and receiver.
4. Simple and easy to use.
5. Fast, inexpensive, safe and secure, accessible.

(a) How to Get Started:

1. Register mobile number with respective bank.
2. Generate MMID. MMID is 7-digit number, to be issued by the bank to the customer upon registration.
3. Get M-PIN. M-PIN is Mobile Banking PIN—secret password—to be used by customer during transaction for authentication and security.
4. Download mobile banking application or use SMS/USSD facility as provided by the bank to make payment.

B. IMPS Funds Transfer through Account Number or IFSC: Currently, IMPS person-to-person funds transfer requires the remitter customer to make funds transfer using beneficiary mobile number and MMID. Both remitter as well as beneficiary needs to register their mobile number with their respective banks and get MMID, in order to send/receive funds using IMPS. There may be cases where remitter is enabled on mobile banking, but beneficiary mobile number is not registered with the bank account. In such cases, remitter shall not be able to send money to the beneficiary.

As per the feedback received from the banking community, the IMPS funds transfer shall now be possible using beneficiary account number and IFS code as well, in addition to beneficiary mobile number and MMID.

C. IMPS Funds Transfer through Internet Banking Channel: IMPS funds transfer can be done through internet banking channels, in addition to mobile phones. The authentication will be done for the remitting customers as (user ID + internet banking password/transaction password) with appropriate existing two-factor authentication method. Since the transaction would be initiated on internet platform, the transaction limits of individual banks for internet channel shall apply. IMPS system is used for beneficiary identification and real-time settlement of transactions.

D. IMPS Funds Transfer through ATM: IMPS funds transfer can be done through ATM, in addition to mobile phones. The authentication will be done for the remitting customers as (card + ATM pin) with appropriate existing two-factor authentication method. Since the transaction would be initiated on ATM, the transaction limits of individual banks for ATM shall apply. IMPS system is used for beneficiary identification and real-time settlement of transactions.

E. IMPS Merchant Payments: IMPS merchant payments (P2M—Person-to-merchant) service allows customers to make instant, 24x7, inter-bank payments to merchants or enterprises via mobile phone. IMPS enables mobile banking users a facility to make payment to merchants and enterprises, through various access channels such as internet, mobile internet, IVR, SMS, USSD.

Customer can make payment to any kind of merchant using IMPS merchant payments service:

1. Mobile top-up/DTH top-up.
2. Insurance premium payment.
3. Online shopping.
4. Over-the-counter payments.

5. Fees payments to schools/colleges/universities.
6. Utility bill payments.
7. Travel and ticketing.

The key features of IMPS merchant payments service are as follows:

1. Instant inter-bank fund transfer.
2. Merchant needs to get on-board IMPS network with one bank. Customer of any bank in the IMPS merchant network can make payment to merchant through IMPS.
3. Convenient and time-saving.
4. Anytime, anywhere service.
5. Safe and secure.
6. 24x7x365 availability.
7. Instant confirmation to sender and receiver.

This service is offered by National Payments Corporation of India (NPCI) in collaboration with member banks.

F. National Unified USSD Platform (NUUP): NUUP offered on a short code *99# is a service which would take banking services to every common man in this country. The service would allow every banking customer to access banking services with a single number across all banks irrespective of the telecom service provider, mobile handset make or the region.

A common platform for all banks instead of each bank having to develop a platform is a strategic move by NPCI to help banks and let them focus on customers to enable this service while NPCI manages the technology behind the platform.

(a) Benefits of NUUP:

1. *99# one number for every Indian to access banking services.
2. 90 percent of phones used in the country are GSM phones and this service works on all GSM phones irrespective of handset make, cost, operating system or even the telecom service provider.
3. Works on basic voice connectivity—unlike an application GPRS connectivity is not required.
4. Customer need not download any application on the phone.

5. Question and answer driven interaction—simple for everyone to understand

(b) Benefits to the Bank:

1. *99# service can be used at BC POS terminals to serve the rural populace.
2. Access to all telecom service providers through a single integration with National Payments Corporation of India.
3. Easier adoption to mobile banking due to simplicity of service and technology.
4. Easier to promote a single code *99# for banking services across all banks.

G. Aadhaar-based Remittance Service (ABRS): In ABRS, a remitter can initiate IMPS transaction using the beneficiary's Aadhaar number, which acts as a financial address and which will be linked to the beneficiaries account number. ABRS facilitates in simplifying the IMPS payment initiation process as in this service the customer will have to input only Aadhaar number of the beneficiary for initiating an IMPS transaction. Another important utility of this service will be in disbursal of subsidy payment i.e. electronic benefit transfer (EBT)/direct benefit transfer (DBT) by the Government. ABRS will act as a catalyst in expanding the financial inclusion reach.

5.4 National Automated Clearing House (NACH)

National Payments Corporation of India (NPCI) has implemented "National Automated Clearing House (NACH)" for banks, financial institutions, corporates and Government—a web-based solution to facilitate inter-bank, high volume, electronic transactions which are repetitive and periodic in nature. NACH System can be used for making bulk transactions towards distribution of subsidies, dividends, interest, salary, pension etc. and also for bulk transactions towards collection of payments pertaining to telephone, electricity, water, loans, investments in mutual funds, insurance premium etc.

National Automated Clearing House (NACH) is a centralised system, launched with an aim to consolidate multiple ECS systems running across the country and provides a framework for the harmonization of standards and practices and removes local barriers/inhibitors. NACH system will provide a national footprint and is expected to cover the entire core banking enabled bank branches spread across the geography of the country irrespective of the location of the bank branch.

With the implementation of NACH system, NPCI intends to provide a single set of rules (operating and business), open standards and best industry practices for electronic transactions which are common across all the participants, service providers and users etc. NACH system also supports financial inclusion measures initiated by Government, Government agencies and banks by providing support to Aadhaar-based transactions.

The NACH system facilitates the member banks to design their own products and also addresses specific needs of the banks and corporates including a refined mandate management system (MMS) and an online dispute management system (DMS) coupled with strong information exchange and customised MIS capabilities.

The NACH system provides a robust, secure and scalable platform to the participants with both transaction and file based transaction processing capabilities. It has best in class security features, cost efficiency and payment performance (STP) coupled with multi-level data validation facility accessible to all participants across the country.

NACH's Aadhaar Payment Bridge (APB) System, developed by NPCI has been helping the Government and Government agencies in making the Direct Benefit Transfer scheme a success. APB System has been successfully channelizing the Government subsidies and benefits to the intended beneficiaries using the Aadhaar numbers. The APB system links the Government departments and their sponsor banks on one side and beneficiary banks and beneficiary on the other side.

5.5 Cheque Truncation System

5.5.1 What is Cheque Truncation? Truncation is the process of stopping the flow of the physical cheque issued by a drawer to the drawee branch. The physical instrument will be truncated at some point enroute to the drawee branch and an electronic image of the cheque would be sent to the drawee branch along with the relevant information like the MICR fields, date of presentation, presenting banks etc. Thus, with the implementation of cheque truncation, the need to move the physical instruments across branches would not be required, except in exceptional circumstances. This would effectively reduce the time required for payment of cheques, the associated cost of transit and delay in processing, etc., thus speeding up the process of collection or realization of the cheques.

5.5.2 Why Cheque Truncation in India? Cheque truncation speeds up collection of cheques and therefore enhances customer service, reduces the scope for clearing related frauds, minimizes cost of collection of cheques, reduces reconciliation problems, eliminates logistics problems etc. With the other major product offering in the form of RTGS, the RBI created the capability to enable inter-bank payments online real time and facilitate corporate customer payments. The other product, national electronic funds transfer, is an electronic credit transfer system.

However, to wish away cheques is simply not possible and that is the reason why the Bank decided to focus on improving the efficiency of the cheque clearing cycle. Cheque truncation is the alternative. Moreover contrary to perceptions, cheque truncation is a more secure system than the current exchange of physical documents in which the cheque moves from one point to another, thus, not only creating delays but inconvenience to the customer in case the instrument is lost in transit or manipulated during the clearing cycle.

In addition to operational efficiency, cheque truncation has several benefits to the banks and customers which includes introduction of new products, re-engineering the total receipts and payments mechanism of the customers, human resource rationalization, cost effectiveness etc. Cheque truncation thus is an important efficiency enhancement initiative in the payment systems area, undertaken by RBI.

5.6 Aadhaar-enabled Payment System (AEPS)

5.6.1 Background: In order to further speed track financial inclusion in the country, two working groups were constituted by the RBI on Micro ATM standards and Central Infrastructure and Connectivity for Aadhaar-based financial inclusion transactions with members representing RBI, Unique Identification Authority of India, NPCI, Institute for Development and Research in Banking Technology and some special invitees representing banks and research institutions.

The working group on Micro ATM Standards and Central Infrastructure and Connectivity has submitted its report to the RBI. As a part of the working group, it was proposed to conduct a lab level proof of concept (PoC), integrating the authentication and encryption standards of UIDAI, to test the efficacy of micro ATM standards and transactions using Aadhaar before they are put to actual use. The PoC was successfully demonstrated at various venues.

AEPS is a bank led model which allows online interoperable financial inclusion transaction at PoS (micro ATM) through the business correspondent of any bank using the Aadhaar authentication.

The four Aadhaar-enabled basic types of banking transactions are as follows:

1. Balance enquiry.
2. Cash withdrawal.
3. Cash deposit.
4. Aadhaar to Aadhaar funds transfer.

The only inputs required for a customer to do a transaction under this scenario are as under:

1. IIN (identifying the bank to which the customer is associated).
2. Aadhaar number.
3. Fingerprint captured during their enrolment.

5.6.2 Objectives:

1. To empower a bank customer to use Aadhaar as his/her identity to access his/her respective Aadhaar enabled bank account and perform basic banking transactions like balance enquiry, cash deposit, cash withdrawal, remittances that are intra-bank or inter-bank in nature, through a business correspondent.
2. To sub-serve the goal of Government of India and RBI in furthering financial inclusion.
3. To sub-serve the goal of RBI in electronification of retail payments.
4. To enable banks to route the Aadhaar initiated inter-bank transactions through a central switching and clearing agency.
5. To facilitate DBT [1] of Government entitlements like NREGA, social security pension, handicapped old age pension etc. of any Central or State Government bodies, using Aadhaar and authentication thereof as supported by the UIDAI.
6. To facilitate inter-operability across banks in a safe and secured manner.
7. To build the foundation for a full range of Aadhaar-enabled banking services.

5.6.3 Services Offered by AEPS:

1. Balance enquiry.
2. Cash withdrawal.
3. Cash deposit.
4. Aadhaar to Aadhaar fund transfer.
5. Gateway authentication service.

Aadhaar is a unique identification number issued by the Unique Identification Authority of India (UIDAI) to residents of India.

Any resident of India holding an Aadhaar number and having a bank account may be a part of the Aadhaar-enabled Payment System. Also, the customer needs to have a bank account for availing AEPS.

Customer should have an Aadhaar (unique ID as issued by UIDAI) number linked with any bank account (bank should be a part of AEPS network) where customer has an account. The registration process shall be as per the procedures laid down by the bank providing AEPS service.

A customer may visit a business correspondent (BC) customer access point. The BC [2] using the point of sale (micro ATM) device will be able to process transactions like cash withdrawal, cash deposit, balance enquiry and fund transfer by selecting the transaction of their choice. The customer needs to provide his Aadhaar number and his bank name or bank IIN number. [3]

A point of sale (PoS) (micro ATM) device is used to facilitate customers to make cash deposit, cash withdrawal, fund transfer and balance enquiry. The PoS device may be a micro ATM.

5.7 RuPay

RuPay, a new card payment scheme launched by NPCI, has been conceived to fulfil RBI's vision to offer a domestic, open-loop, multilateral system which will allow all Indian banks and financial institutions in India to participate in electronic payments.

"RuPay", the word itself has a sense of nationality in it. "RuPay" is the coinage of two terms Rupee and payment. The RuPay visual identity is a modern and dynamic unit. The orange and green arrows indicate a nation on the move and a service that matches its pace. The colour blue stands for the feeling of tranquillity which is the people must get while owning a card of the brand 'RuPay'. The bold and unique typeface grants solidity to the whole unit and symbolizes a stable entity.

RuPay was created to fulfil the RBI's desire to have a domestic, open loop, and multilateral system of payments in India. In India, 90 percent of credit card transactions and almost all debit card transactions are domestic. However, the cost of transactions was high due to monopoly of foreign gateways like Visa and MasterCard. In recent years, the usage of credit and debit cards (called plastic money) has increased manifold. It was thought that if this process of transactions is made India-centric, cost can come down drastically. RuPay facilitates electronic payment at all Indian banks and financial institutions, and competes with MasterCard and Visa in India. NPCI maintains ties with Discover Financial to enable the card scheme to gain international acceptance.

RuPay card was launched on March 26, 2012. NPCI entered into a strategic partnership with Discover Financial Services (DFS) for RuPay Card, enabling the acceptance of RuPay Global Cards on Discover's global payment network outside of India.

RuPay cards are accepted at all ATMs across India under National Financial Switch, and under the NPCI's agreement with DFS, RuPay cards are accepted on the international Discover network. According to the data published by National Payments Corporation of India, there are more than 26,14,584 point of sale (PoS) terminals in India under the RuPay platform. In addition to the ATMs and PoS terminals, RuPay cards are accepted online on 10,000 e-commerce websites.

RuPay cards are accepted at all PoS terminals in India. To enable this, RuPay has certified 39 major banks in India to accept the RuPay card at their respective PoS terminals located at different merchant locations.

5.8 Bharat Interface for Money (BHIM)

It is a mobile app developed by NPCI based on the unified payment interface (UPI). [4] It was launched by Prime Minister Shri Narendra Modi in New Delhi on December 30, 2016. Named after Dr. Bhimrao Ambedkar, it is intended to facilitate e-payments directly through banks and as a part of the drive towards cashless transactions in the wake of demonetization of high value currency notes in November 2016.

This UPI app supports all Indian banks which use that platform, which is built over the *immediate payment service* infrastructure and allows the user to instantly transfer money between the bank accounts of any two parties. It can be used on all mobile devices.

5.9 Aadhaar Payment Bridge (APB) System

It is a unique payment system implemented by National Payments Corporation of India (NPCI), which uses Aadhaar number as a central key for electronically channelizing the Government subsidies and benefits in the Aadhaar-enabled Bank Accounts (AEBA) of the intended beneficiaries. It is a payment system based on Aadhaar numbers issued by UIDAI and IIN (Institution Identification Number) issued by NPCI. APB System is used by the Government departments and agencies for the transfer of benefits and subsidies under Direct Benefit Transfer (DBT) scheme launched by Government of India.

The APB System sub-serves the goal of financial inclusion and provides an opportunity to the Government to attempt financial re-engineering of its subsidy management program. The implementation of APB System has also lead to electronification of a large number of retail payment transactions which were predominantly either in cash or cheque.

APB System eliminates inordinate delays, multiple channels and paperwork involved in the existing system and transfers benefits and subsidies in a seamless and timely manner and directly into the Aadhaar-enabled Bank Account. In case of change in bank account, customer is not required to convey the bank account detailsϖ or change in bank details to the Government department or agency. Customer is also not required to open multiple bank accounts for receiving benefits and subsidies of various social welfare schemes. A customer just needs to open one account and seed his/her Aadhaar number in the bank account to start receiving benefits and subsidies directly into his/her Aadhaar-enabled Bank Account.

Endnotes

1. Direct Benefit Transfer (DBT) is a scheme launched by Government of India to transfer the benefits and subsidies of various social welfare schemes like LPG subsidy, MGNREGA payments, old age pension, scholarships etc. directly in the bank account of the beneficiary.
2. Business correspondent (BC) is an approved bank agent providing basic banking service using a micro ATM (terminal) to any bank customer wishing to avail their bank BC service.
3. IIN identifies the bank with which a customer has mapped his Aadhaar number. IIN is a six digit number. In most banks' BC customer service points, this number would be represented on the terminal by the banks logo or name.
4. Unified payment interface (UPI) of India is a payment system which facilitates the fund transfer between two bank accounts. This payment system works on the mobile platform. Sending money through the UPI app is as easy as sending a message. The customer is not required to give bank account details for the funds transfer through the UPI payment system.

6

Some Other Forms of Retail Payments

The retail payment systems in India also consist of the paper-based clearing systems, electronic clearing systems and those systems relating to payment cards (credit and debit).

6.1 Paper-based Systems (Cheques)

Cheques as payment instruments are the most popular mode of non-cash payment in India. The clearing and settlement of cheques drawn on different banks require the coming together of the banks in that area for transfer of instruments and the final settlement of funds. This process is facilitated by the clearing houses at these centres. As on March 31, 2018, there were 1,051 operational clearing houses. Of these, 3 are cheque truncation system (CTS) grids managed by the RBI which handle the cheque clearing volumes of erstwhile 66 MICR CPCs. The reaming 1,048 are non-MICR clearing houses. The clearing and settlement cycle is completed in two days—on day 1, the cheques are presented at the clearing house and on day 2, the funds settlement and return clearing are accounted for.

As at end-march 2018, paper-based systems constituted a miniscule portion of retail payment systems in India (7.4 percent). Interestingly, due to steps taken by the RBI to encourage electronic transactions, the number of clearing houses declined from 1,373 as on March 31, 2014 to 1,051 as on March 31, 2018.

The introduction of (CTS) was yet another step for increasing the efficiency of retail payment system. Truncation is the process of stopping the flow of the physical cheque issued by a drawer at some point with the presenting bank enroute to the drawee bank branch. In its place, an electronic image of the cheque is transmitted to the drawee branch by the clearing house, along with relevant information like data on the MICR band, date of presentation, presenting bank, etc.

The RBI implemented the CTS in the National Capital Region (NCR), New Delhi, Chennai and Mumbai with effect from February 1, 2008, September 24, 2011 and April 27, 2013 respectively. After migration of the entire cheque volume from MICR system to CTS, the traditional MICR-based cheque processing has been discontinued in the country. Based on the advantages realised by the stakeholders and the experienced gained from the roll-out in these centres, it was decided to operationalise CTS across the country. The new approach envisioned as part of the national roll-out is the grid-based approach.

Under this approach, the entire cheque volume in the country which was earlier cleared through 66 MICR cheque processing locations is consolidated into the three grids in New Delhi, Chennai and Mumbai. Each grid provides processing and clearing services to all the banks under its respective jurisdiction.

Under grid-based cheque truncation system clearing, all cheques drawn on bank branches falling within in the grid jurisdiction are treated and cleared as local cheques.

6.2 Electronic Retail Payment Instruments

6.2.1 Benefits of Electronic Payments: These are as under:

A. Common Man: (a) Reduced cash and hence more safety, (b) faster payment, (c) reduced number of visits to bank, and (d) interest earning on money in the bank.

B. Vendors: (a) Transactions settled quickly, (b) getting rid of coins and change, (c) larger transactions made easy, (d) improved accounting and book keeping, (e) no need to keep large amounts of cash.

The electronic retail payment systems in India are national electronic funds transfer (NEFT) system and the electronic clearing service (ECS).

6.2.2 National Electronic Funds Transfer (NEFT): Electronic Funds Transfer (EFT) system was introduced in the mid-1990s. EFT facilitates transfer of funds from one bank account to another. In the beginning EFT system was permitted only for government transactions and RBI-initiated payments. NEFT is an electronic message-based payment system, and was introduced by the RBI in November 2005 to replace the EFT system which was public key infrastructure (PKI)-enabled and the settlements were effected on a decentralized mode.

NEFT is more secure, nation-wide retail electronic payment system to facilitate funds transfer by the bank customers, between the networked bank branches in the country. This has facilitated the availability of electronic payment modes at more centres. There are 23 daily settlements during weekdays.

The banks are to credit the accounts of the customers for the first four settlements on the same day and for the fifth and sixth settlements, the customers' accounts are to be credited not later than T+1 (next working day).

As on March 31, 2018, NEFT was available at 1,40,339 branches all over the country with 192 participating banks.

In order to popularise the e-payments in the country, the RBI, on its part, waived the service charges to be levied on the member banks, till March 31, 2009, in respect of the real time gross settlement (RTGS) and NEFT transactions. The RBI also provided, free of charge, intra-day liquidity to the banks for the RTGS transactions.

The service charges to be levied by banks from their customers for RTGS and NEFT were however deregulated and left to the discretion of the individual banks. While some of the banks rationalised their service charges and a few had made it even cost-free to the customers, there were certain banks that had fixed unreasonably high service charges for providing these services to their customers.

In its latest notification dated June 11, 2019, the RBI decided that with effect from July 1, 2019, processing charges and time varying charges levied on banks by RBI for outward transactions undertaken using the RTGS system, as also the processing charges levied by RBI for transactions processed in NEFT system will be waived by the RBI. The RBI also advised the banks to pass on this benefit to customers using RTGS and NEFT with effect from July 1, 2019.

6.2.3 Electronic Clearing Services (ECS): ECS is a retail payment system which facilitates bulk payments that can be classified as one-to-many and receipts that are many-to-one. The two components of this system are ECS (Credit) and ECS (Debit). This facility is now available at 91 major centres.

- **ECS (Credit):** It facilitates the bulk payments whereby the account of the institution remitting the payment is debited and the payments remitted to beneficiaries' accounts. This facility is mostly used for making multiple payments, like payment of dividend to investors, payment of salaries of employees by institutions etc. For this purpose, the company or entity making the payment has to have the bank account details of the individual beneficiaries.
- **ECS (Debit):** It facilitates the collection of payments by utility companies. In this system the account of the customers of the utility company in different banks are debited and the amounts are transferred to the account of the utility company. The company providing this facility has to receive the mandate to collect funds from its customer. On receipt of the mandate, the company advises the consumer's bank to debit the payment due from the account on the due dates.

Settlement in this system currently takes place on T+0 basis and the cycle gets completed on T+1 basis. The clearing and settlement transactions through ECS occur at the respective centres. A centralised facility is available at the RBI, Mumbai to receive the ECS (Credit) files meant for credit at the other 14 RBI centres.

6.3 Credit/Debit Cards

In recent years advancements in banking technology,

progress in mobile banking and innovative technologies to facilitate digital payments have enabled large number of small denomination transactions to be handled smoothly in electronic mode. The Government of India has taken policy decisions to encourage cashless/electronic transactions. In its endeavour on moving towards electronic payments, the Central Government has announced a number of incentives.

A credit card is a payment card issued to users (cardholders) to enable the cardholder to pay a merchant for goods and services, based on the cardholder's promise to the card issuer to pay them for the amounts so paid plus other agreed charges. The card issuer (usually a bank) creates a revolving account and grants a line of credit to the cardholder, from which the cardholder can borrow money for payment to a merchant or as a cash advance.

A debit card is a plastic payment card that can be used instead of cash when making purchases. It is similar to a credit card, but unlike a credit card, the money comes directly from the user's bank account when performing a transaction.

There has been phenomenal increase in the number of credit cards issued by the banks in India during the last few years. The number of outstanding credit cards at end-April 2019 stood at over 4.80 crore.

While the increasing usage of the credit cards is a welcome development in as much as it reduces reliance on currency for settlement of transactions, it also entails certain additional elements of operational risk and can be a potential source of customer complaints.

In order to ensure orderly growth of the card segment of consumer credit and protect the interests of banks/non-banking financial companies (NBFCs) and their customers, the RBI constituted a Working Group on Regulatory Mechanism for Cards (Chairman: R. Gandhi).

Based of the recommendations of the Working Group, draft guidelines on credit cards were framed by the RBI in June 2005 for all commercial banks/NBFCs with regard to their credit card operations.

The draft guidelines delineated the broad parameters that banks/NBFCs should, at the minimum, take into account with regard to the following:

1. Issue of cards with respect to clear mentioning of most important terms and conditions (MITCs).
2. Interest rates and other charges on customers.
3. Corrective mechanism on account of wrongful billing.
4. Use of direct sale agents and other agents for outsourcing various credit card operations.
5. Protection of customer rights especially in respect of right to privacy, customer confidentiality and fair practices in debt collection.
6. Redressal avenues of customer grievances.
7. Internal control and monitoring systems of the banks/NBFCs for such card operations.

The draft guidelines further stipulated that each bank/NBFC must have a well-documented policy and a *fair practices code* for credit card operations. The *fair practices code* for credit card operations released by the IBA in March 2005 could also be used by banks/NBFCs. The bank/NBFCs code should, at the minimum, however, incorporate the relevant guidelines contained in the draft guidelines released by the RBI.

6.4 ATM Networks

The main advantage of an ATM network is that it obviates the need for having bank-specific multiple ATM installations in the same geographical area, thereby reducing the entailed costs for the banks but without compromising on the reach of the banks to their customers.

Over the years, the relative growth in off-site ATMs has been much more than that of on-site ATMs. As a result, by end-April 2019, off-site ATMs accounted for approximately 47.06 percent (97,487) of the total ATMs in the country. With the policy initiative to enable non-bank entities to set up and operate ATMs—White Label ATMs (WLAs)—the proportion of off-site ATMs is likely to grow further.

The National Financial Switch (NFS) network started its operations on August 27, 2004. NFS is one of the several shared ATM networks which inter-connect the ATM switches of the banks together and thus enable inter-operability of the ATM cards issued by any bank across the entire network. The Board for Regulation and Supervision of Payment and Settlement systems (BPSS) approved in-principle to issue authorisation to National Payments Corporation of India (NPCI) for operating various retail payment systems in the country. RBI has also issued authorisation to NPCI to take over the operations of National Financial Switch (NFS) from the Institute of Development and Research in Banking Technology (IDRBT) on October 15, 2009. NPCI took over NFS operations from December 14, 2009. Use of the ATMs connected through any of the ATM networks in the country became cost free for the customers from April 1, 2009.

As at end-April 2019, the number of ATMs in the country stood at 2,07,131.

6.5 Digital Wallet

Digital wallet refers to an electronic device that allows an individual to make electronic transactions. This can include purchasing items online with a computer or using a smart phone to purchase something at a store. An individual's bank account can also be linked to the digital wallet. He may also have his driver's license, health card, loyalty card(s) and other ID documents stored on the phone. The credentials can be passed to a merchant's terminal wirelessly via near field communication (NFC). Increasingly, digital wallets are being made not just for basic financial transactions but to also authenticate the holder's credentials. For example, a digital wallet could potentially verify the age of the buyer to the store while purchasing alcohol. The system has already gained popularity in Japan, where digital wallets are known as "wallet mobiles".

A digital wallet has both a software and information

component. The software provides security and encryption for the personal information and for the actual transaction. Typically, digital wallets are stored on the client side and are easily self-maintained and fully compatible with most e-commerce websites. A server-side digital wallet, also known as a thin wallet, is one that an organization creates for and about you and maintains on its servers. Server-side digital wallets are gaining popularity among major retailers due to the security, efficiency, and added utility it provides to the end-user, which increases their satisfaction of their overall purchase. The information component is basically a database of user-input information. This information consists of your shipping address, billing address, payment methods (including credit card numbers, expiry dates, and security numbers), and other information.

Digital wallet systems enable the widespread use of digital wallet transactions among various retail vendors in the form of mobile payments systems and digital wallet applications.

A client-side digital wallet requires minimal set-up and is relatively easy to use. Once the software is installed, the user begins by entering all the pertinent information. The digital wallet is now set up. At the purchase or check-out page of an e-commerce site, the digital wallet software has the ability to automatically enter the user information in the online form. By default, most digital wallets prompt when the software recognizes a form in which it can fill out; if one chooses to fill out the form automatically, the user will be prompted for a password. This keeps unauthorized users away from viewing personal information stored on a particular computer.

6.5.1 Application of Digital Wallets: Consumers are not required to fill out order forms on each site when they purchase an item because the information has already been stored and is automatically updated and entered into the order fields across merchant sites when using a digital wallet. Consumers also benefit when using digital wallets because their information is encrypted or protected by a private software code; merchants benefit by receiving protection against fraud.

Digital wallets are available to consumers free of charge, and they are fairly easy to obtain. For example, when a consumer makes a purchase at a merchant site that is set up to handle server-side digital wallets, he types his name and payment and shipping information into the merchant's own form. At the end of the purchase, the consumer is asked to sign up for a wallet of his choice by entering a user name and password for future purchases. Users can also acquire wallets at a wallet vendor's site.

Although a wallet is free for consumers, vendors charge merchants for wallets. Some wallet vendors make arrangements for merchants to pay them a percentage of every successful purchase directed through their wallets. In other cases, digital wallet vendors process the transactions between cardholders and participating merchants and charge merchants a flat fee.

6.5.2 Advantages for E-commerce Sites: Many online shoppers abandon their order due to frustration in filling in forms. The digital wallet combats this problem by giving users the option to transfer their information securely and accurately. This simplified approach to completing transactions results in better usability and ultimately more utility for the customer.

Digital wallets can also increase the security of the transaction since the wallet typically does not pass payment card details to the website (a unique transaction identifier or token is shared instead). Increasingly this approach is a feature of online payment gateways, especially if the payment gateway offers a *hosted payment page* integration approach.

6.6 Deficiencies in Retail Payment Systems

The deficiencies in retail payments mainly pertain to the inefficient outstation cheque collection process. In this regard, it is difficult to prescribe a standard time-frame for collection in view of large disparities at various centres, in terms of their location, availability of infrastructure, communication facilities, etc. In respect of metropolitan cities, State capitals and A class cities, most banks have a policy of collecting instruments within a period of 7 to 10 days. In respect of other cities including States in the North-Eastern region, most banks have declared in their policies that the instruments will be collected within a maximum period of 14 days.

The usage of ECS has seen rapid increase. The main deficiency in ECS system has been the decentralised model of transaction processing in the system. While a centralised ECS has been provided, this is available only at the RBI centres. To address this deficiency, a National Electronic Clearing Platform was implemented in September 2008.

The benefits of electronic payment infrastructure are not yet trickling down to the lower end of the customer segment which still largely uses services like money order and informal channels for transferring money of small value which has much higher cost and time lag for transferring money. There is a need to develop solutions using newer technologies which would allow all segments of the society to gain access to the benefits offered by these facilities.

In order to popularise e-payments in the country, the RBI, on its part, has decided to waive off, with effect from July 1, 2019, processing charges and time varying charges levied on banks by RBI for outward transactions undertaken using the RTGS system, as also the processing charges levied by RBI for transactions processed in NEFT system will be waived by the RBI.

The RBI also advised the banks to pass on this benefit to customers using RTGS and NEFT with effect from July 1, 2019.

7

Payment Banks

In 2007, European Union (EU) adopted the Payment Services Directive (PSD) for a harmonised legal framework for retail payment services. The PSD contains both prudential requirements and civil law provisions pertaining to the various payment service providers and the payment services they provide. To promote competition, a new group of payment service providers, the so-called payment institutions, has been created. They can offer payment services without being a bank and do not have to cover the entire range of services provided by a bank. In addition, the rules pertaining to the execution of transactions have been clearly defined. In Japan, non-banks are allowed to provide funds transfers. In South Africa, non-banks can become designated clearing system participants and have full access to the clearing system.

Taking into account the need to urgently provide access to payment services and deposit products to millions of individuals, experts proposed that a set of banks may be licensed under the Banking Regulation Act, which may be referred to as payment banks. Potential candidates for such a license could include separately capitalised subsidiaries of non-banking financial companies (NBFCs), existing corporate business correspondents (BCs), mobile phone companies, consumer goods companies, the post office system, and real sector cooperatives.

7.1 Payment Banks: Background

On September 23, 2013, Committee on Comprehensive Financial Services for Small Businesses and Low Income Households (Chairman: Nachiket Mor), was formed by the Reserve Bank of India (RBI). On January 7, 2014, the Committee submitted its final report. Among its various recommendations, it recommended the formation of a new category of banks called payment banks. On July 17, 2014, the RBI released the draft guidelines for payment banks, seeking comments for interested entities and the general public. On November 27, 2014 the RBI released the final guidelines for payment banks.

It may be recalled that in the Union Budget 2014-2015 presented on July 10, 2014, the Finance Minister had announced, "After making suitable changes to current framework, a structure will be put in place for continuous authorization of universal banks in the private sector in the current financial year. RBI will create a framework for licensing small banks and other differentiated banks. Differentiated banks serving niche interests, local area banks, payment banks etc. are contemplated to meet credit and remittance needs of small businesses, unorganized sector, low income households, farmers and migrant work force".

7.2 Guidelines for Licensing of Payment Banks

RBI released on November 27, 2014, the following guidelines for licensing of payments banks.

7.2.1 Objective: The objective of setting up of payments banks is to further financial inclusion by providing: (a) small savings accounts and (b) payments/remittance services to migrant labour workforce, low income households, small businesses, other unorganised sector entities and other users.

7.2.2 Eligible Promoters: Existing non-bank pre-paid payment instrument (PPI) issuers and other entities—such as individuals/professionals, non-banking finance companies (NBFCs), corporate business correspondents (BCs), mobile telephone companies, super-market chains, companies, real sector cooperatives—that are owned and controlled by residents; and public sector entities may apply to set up payments banks.

A promoter/promoter group can have a joint venture with an existing scheduled commercial bank to set up a payments bank. However, scheduled commercial bank can take equity stake in a payments bank to the extent permitted under Section 19(2) of the Banking Regulation Act, 1949.

Promoter/promoter groups should be *fit and proper* with a sound track record of professional experience or running their businesses for at least a period of 5 years in order to be eligible to promote payments banks.

7.2.3 Scope of Activities: As regards acceptance of demand deposits, payment banks will initially be restricted to holding a maximum balance of ₹ 1,00,000 per individual customer. However, it may be raised by the RBI based on the performance of the bank.

Payments banks cannot issue credit cards. Payments and remittance services will be provided through various channels.

25 percent of the branches of a payment bank must be in the unbanked rural area. The bank must use the term *payments bank* to differentiate it from other types of banks. The bank will be licensed as payments bank under Section 22 of the Banking Regulation Act, 1949, and will be registered as a public limited company under the Companies Act, 2013.

7.2.4 Deployment of Funds: Payment banks cannot undertake lending activities. Apart from amounts maintained as cash reserve ratio (CRR) with the RBI on its outside demand and time liabilities, payment banks will be required to invest minimum 75 percent of their *demand deposit balances* in statutory liquidity ratio (SLR) eligible Government securities/treasury bills with maturity up to 1 year and hold maximum 25 percent in current and time/fixed deposits with other scheduled commercial banks for operational purposes and liquidity management.

7.2.5 Capital Requirement: The minimum paid-up equity capital for payment banks is ₹ 100 crore. Payments banks should have a leverage ratio of not less than 3 percent, i.e. their outside liabilities should not exceed 33.33 times their net worth (paid-up capital and reserves).

7.2.6 Promoter's Contribution: Promoter's minimum initial contribution to the paid-up equity capital of such payment banks shall, at least, be 40 percent for the first five years from the commencement of the business.

7.2.7 Foreign Shareholding: Foreign shareholding in the payment banks would be as per the foreign direct investment (FDI) policy for private sector banks as amended from time to time.

7.2.8 Voting Rights: The voting rights will be regulated by the Banking Regulation Act, 1949. The voting right of any shareholder is capped at 10 percent, which can be raised to 26 percent by RBI. Any acquisition of more than 5 percent will require approval of the RBI. The majority of the bank's board of directors should consist of independent directors, appointed according to RBI guidelines.

7.2.9 Other Conditions: Operations of the bank should be fully networked and technology driven from the beginning, conforming to generally accepted standards and norms. The bank can accept utility bills. It cannot form subsidiaries to undertake non-banking activities. The bank should have a high powered customer grievances cell to handle customer complaints.

7.2.10 Procedure for Application: In terms of Rule 11 of the Banking Regulation (Companies) Rules, 1949, applications shall be submitted in the prescribed form (Form III) to the Chief General Manager, Department of Banking Regulation, Reserve Bank of India, Mumbai. In addition, the applicants should furnish the business plan and other requisite information as indicated. Applications will be accepted till the close of business as on January 16, 2015. After experience gained in dealing with payments banks, applications will be received on a continuous basis. However, these guidelines are subject to periodic review and revision.

7.2.11 Procedure for RBI Decisions: An External Advisory Committee (EAC) comprising eminent professionals like bankers, chartered accountants, finance professionals etc. will evaluate the applications. The decision to issue an in-principle approval for setting up of a bank will be taken by the

RBI. Decision of the RBI in this regard will be final.

The validity of the in-principle approval issued by the RBI will be 18 months. The names of applicants for bank licences will be placed on the website of RBI.

In February 2015, RBI released the list of entities which had applied for a payment bank licence. There were 41 applicants. It was also announced that an external advisory committee (EAC) headed by Nachiket Mor would evaluate the licence applications.

EAC submitted its findings on July 6, 2015. The applicant entities were examined for their financial track record and governance issues. On August 19, 2015, the RBI gave *in-principle* licences to the following 11 entities to launch payment banks:

1. Aditya Birla Nuvo.
2. Airtel M Commerce Services.
3. Cholamandalam Distribution Services.
4. Department of Posts.
5. FINO PayTech.
6. National Securities Depository.
7. Reliance Industries.
8. Dilip Shanghvi, Sun Pharmaceuticals.
9. Vijay Shekhar Sharma, Paytm.
10. Tech Mahindra.
11. Vodafone M-Pesa.

The *in-principle* license was valid for 18 months within which the entities were to fulfil the requirements. They were not allowed to engage in banking activities within the period. The RBI would consider grant of full licenses under Section 22 of the Banking Regulation Act, 1949, after it was satisfied that the conditions had been fulfilled.

On February 28, 2015, during the presentation of the Union Budget it was announced that India Post [1] will use its large network to run payment banks. On June 1, 2016, Union Cabinet cleared the proposal to set up postal payment banks. There are 1,54,000 post offices in the country out of which 1,39,000 are in rural areas. 650 branches of postal payment banks will be established in the country and linked to rural post offices. By September 2017, all 650 branches of postal payment banks will become operational.

Thus, payment bank is a new model of banks conceptualised by the Reserve Bank of India (RBI). These banks can accept a restricted deposit, which is currently limited to ₹ 1 lakh per customer and may be increased further. These banks cannot issue loans and credit cards. Both current account and savings accounts can be operated by such banks. Payments banks can issue services like ATM cards, debit cards, net banking and mobile banking. Bharti Airtel set up India's first live payments bank.

According to RBI, the objective of setting up of payment banks is to further financial inclusion by providing: (a) small savings accounts and (b) payments/remittance services to migrant labour workforce, low income households, small businesses, other unorganised sector entities and other user.

7.3 India Post Payments Bank (IPPB)

IPPB is a Government of India owned payment bank, operating under the Department of Posts, Ministry of Communication, which aims to utilize all of India's 1,55,015 post offices as access points and 3,00,000 postal service workers to provide house-to-house banking services. The first phase of the bank with 650 branches and 3250 post offices as access points was inaugurated on September 1, 2018 by Prime Minister Shri Narendra Modi. Over 10,000 postmen have been roped into the first phase.

On August 19, 2015, India Post got licence to run a payment bank from Reserve Bank of India. On August 17, 2016 it was registered as a public limited government company for setting up a payment bank. The pilot project of IPPB was inaugurated on January 30, 2017 at Raipur and Ranchi. In August 2018, the Union Cabinet approved ₹ 1,435 crore for setting up the bank. The first phase nationwide inauguration happened on

September 1, 2018.

IPPB offers savings accounts, money transfer and insurances through third parties, bill and utility payments. It will reach to rural and far-flung areas of the country, delivering banking services to the doorstep of every Indian.

- The bank offers savings and current accounts up to a balance of ₹ 1 lakh.
- Customers can use QR code payments eliminating the need to remember account numbers, PINs and passwords.
- Unified payments interface.
- Immediate payment service.
- NEFT.
- RTGS.
- Bharat BillPay.
- Direct benefit transfer.

IPPB has been allowed to link around 17 crore postal savings bank (PSB) accounts with its accounts. The Government aims to link all the 1,55,000 post offices to the IPPB system by December 31, 2018.

IPPB will use Aadhaar to open accounts, while a QR card and biometrics will drive authentication, transactions, and payments.

The Government owns 100 percent in IPPB, which has been set up under the aegis of the Department of Posts, and will offer products and services though multiple channels such as counter services, micro ATMs, mobile banking app, messages and interactive voice response.

7.3.1 Main Features of IPPB: These are as under:

1. *Grameen Dak Sewaks* will be armed with smart phones and biometric devices to handle transactions.
2. IPPB will operate like a banking organisation, but with smaller scale operations. Most banking operations like accepting deposits shall be done, but loans cannot be given and credit cards cannot be issued.
3. IPPB can accept deposits of up to ₹ 1 lakh per customer, offer payments and remittance services, mobile

payments/transfers/purchases and other banking services like ATM/debit cards, net banking and third party fund transfers.

4. IPPB has tied-up with PNB and Bajaj Allianz Life Insurance for products such as loans as well as insurance. These facilities can be accessed through 650 branches and 3,250 access points.
5. Around 1,30,000 access points will be located in rural areas to fulfil Government's financial inclusion goal. IPPB also has a nod to link around 17 crore postal savings bank (PSB) accounts with its own set-up.
6. Deposits in any account that exceed ₹ 1 lakh will be automatically converted into post office savings account.
7. IPPB will give different interest rate according to the deposit amount.

- Deposit up to ₹ 25,000—4.5 percent.
- Deposit up to ₹ 50,000—5 percent.
- Up to ₹ 1,00,000—5.5 percent.

8. One can open a zero balance savings account.
9. Existing saving account with the post offices can be converted into IPPB saving account. It would give a better interest rate.
10. The Government is planning to send postman to your home for cash deposit and withdrawals. It would be a charged service.

7.4 Other Prominent Payment Banks in India

7.4.1 Airtel Payment Bank: It is a public limited company with its headquarters in New Delhi. The company is a subsidiary of Bharti Airtel. It is the first company in India to receive a payments bank license from RBI and it became the first live payments bank in the country. On April 11, 2016 RBI issued the license under Section 22(1) of Banking Regulation Act, 1949 to Airtel Payment Bank. It is a joint venture between Bharti Airtel Ltd. and Kotak Mahindra Bank Ltd. Kotak Mahindra Bank holds 19.9 percent stake in the Airtel Payment Bank.

Main features of Airtel Payment Bank are as under:

- The bank supports UPI payment system for funds transfer. The UPI is the most advanced mechanism of funds transfer. It is free, instant and always available.
- It gives a free digital debit card in association with the MasterCard. There is an annual charge for this card.
- The bank opens your account instantly and requires no documents. It only needs your Aadhaar along with the fingerprints.
- Your Airtel number is your bank account number.
- Free personal accident insurance cover of ₹ 1 lakh.

7.4.2 Paytm Payment Bank: Paytm is promoting its payment bank and advising its wallet customers to shift into the payment bank. The bank started its operation in December 2017.

Some features of Paytm Payment Bank are as under:

- It opens a zero balance account.
- Free insurance cover of ₹ 2 lakh.
- Fixed deposit facility in partnership with IndusInd Bank.
- Free digital Rupay debit card.

7.4.3 Fino Payment Bank: Fino Payment Bank has not advertised itself much but it has a strong footing. This bank gives a variety of services which include current and savings accounts, remittances, business correspondent (BC) lending, mobile banking, life and general insurance and bill payments.

Important features of Fino Payment Bank are as follows:

- It has its own branches at 410 places.
- It is present at BPCL petrol pumps.
- The bank has focussed on remittance business.
- It has partnered with the ICICI Bank. ICICI ATMs are installed at Fino branches.
- It also sells auto loans, personal loans and home loans of the ICICI Bank.
- The bank requires ₹ 1,000 minimum balance in the account.

7.4.4 Aditya Birla Idea Payment Bank: The bank started operations from February 22, 2018. However, the details are not out yet. Similarly, Jio Payment Bank is also in the process of establishing itself.

Though not a payment bank, Google Pay (formerly Google Tez) is an online payment app that provides users with an option to send or receive money over unified payments interface (UPI). Unlike traditional payment transfer methods like NEFT and RTGS, UPI makes it easier to send or receive money directly from or to a bank account in real time, just like a text message.

Endnote

1. Department of Posts (India Post) is a department of the Ministry of Communications and Information Technology, Government of India. Postal services in India have touched the lives of every citizen for more than 150 years, be it through mails, banking, insurance, money transfer or retail services.

8

Electronic Money (E-money) and Electronic Commerce (E-commerce)

In recent years, there has been a gradual switchover from the use of paper-based payments media to those based on electronics. While the basic characteristics of these new instruments are by and large similar to those of paper-based instruments, the former present a different set of challenges to policy makers. E-money is one such new product which has appeared on Indian horizon recently.

8.1 Electronic Money (E-money)

8.1.1 Meaning and Kinds of E-money: E-money may be broadly defined as an electronic store of monetary value on a technical device used for making payments to undertakings other than the issuer without necessarily involving bank accounts in the transaction, but acting as a prepaid bearer instrument. E-money can be classified into the following two broad categories:

1. Pre-paid stored value card (also called electronic purse).
2. Pre-paid software-based product that uses computer networks such as internet (also referred to as digital cash or network money).

The stored value card scheme typically uses a microprocessor chip embedded in a plastic card while software based scheme typically uses specialised software installed in a personal computer. The stored value card could be of three types:

1. Single-purpose card.
2. Closed-system or limited-purpose card.
3. General-purpose or multi-purpose card.

The single-purpose card generally with a magnetic chip

recording the amount of fund therein is designed to facilitate only one type of transaction, e.g. telephone calls, public transportation, laundry, parking facilities etc. In this case the distinguishing point is that the issuer and the service provider (acceptor) are identical for the cards. These cards are expected to substitute coins and currency notes.

Closed-system or limited-purpose card is generally used in a small number of well-identified points of sale within a well-identified location such as corporate/university campus.

Multi-purpose card can perform a variety of functions with several vendors, viz. credit card, debit card, stored value card, identification card, repository of personal medical information etc. The importance of these cards is especially underscored with respect to regulatory oversight, restrictions on issuers and their implications for monetary policy. These cards may reduce demand for current accounts in the bank for likely reduction in transaction costs, and prudent portfolio management.

It is important to distinguish here the so-called *access* products, e.g. credit card and debit card from e-money. The former typically require a telephone or a personal computer with appropriate software to access the customer account before transferring the value while under e-money, the amount of value is already embedded and it may be increased or reduced without necessarily involving a personal bank account. In a sense, e-money can be construed as an electronic form of travellers' cheques (TCs). In both cases, the user pays for the instrument upfront.

8.1.2 Benefits of E-money: Use and spread of e-money depends upon the incentives of issuers, merchants and consumers. For issuers, the principal motivation arises from revenues to be earned from investment of outstanding balances (i.e. float income), savings of costs from reduced handling of cash and incentive of offering fee-based service to consumers and merchants besides the larger security emanating from audit trail of transactions and improved management information system.

For merchants, the trade-off would be between reduction in cost of handling physical cash vis-à-vis cost of putting in place necessary infrastructure.

For consumers, the use of e-money would depend upon the perceived security and privacy of e-money and ease with which e-money could be used which would again depend upon willingness of merchants to accept e-money. In other words, apart from security, privacy and ease, network effects are also important for wider use of e-money.

An economy like India, where cash transactions are very high, could benefit from using e-money through cost savings from printing and minting of smaller denomination notes and coins and eliminating the cost of handling, storing, transporting and insuring currency. These should also improve operational efficiency of the financial sector as also extension of banking to the urban poor and rural communities besides facilitating e-governance initiatives of governments. However, such benefits should be weighed against the need to build up the costly infrastructure to operate nationwide cashless retail payment system.

8.1.3 Implications of E-money for the Central Bank: Before analysing the likely implications, it is instructive to note that e-money can be issued in three alternate ways. Each of these three ways may have different implications for conduct of monetary policy.

1. E-money can be issued in exchange of cash (i.e. 100 percent backing of central bank money). Under that circumstance, there may be only marginal change in total money supply in the economy provided there is no significant change in velocity of circulation of money.
2. E-money can also be issued on credit against interest payment.
3. E-money could also be issued as a separate form of currency independent of central bank money by entities other than the central bank. In that case, e-money would compete against the central bank money as a medium of

exchange. However, such a scenario in which public gets e-money from an entity in exchange for something other than the central bank money seems remote now.

Currency notes and coins generally form an overwhelming part of the balance sheet of any central bank. If e-money is extensively used and in the process, replaces substantially central bank's money, central bank's balance sheet would *shrink* while that of the issuing authority of e-money would *expand* in relative terms.

With large scale use of e-money, it is apprehended that central bank's balance sheet may shrink to such an extent relative to that of the banking sector that it may be unable to perform its liquidity absorption function [in effect, open market operations (OMOs)] on account of non-availability of adequate volume of assets. Under that circumstance, extensive e-monetisation in the economy could jeopardise the conduct of monetary policy of the central bank. It may, however, be noted that the central bank would not have any problem in liquidity injection because central bank money is still the only legal tender in the economy.

Apart from constraining its liquidity management function, relative shrinkage in balance sheet may also have implications regarding loss of *seigniorage* revenue for the central bank. This is because currency notes and coins are the interest-free liability of the central bank towards public (i.e. public have in effect lent to the central bank such amount free of interest) which are then used by the central bank to purchase interest bearing assets. Thus, interest earned on these assets constitutes its seigniorage revenue. Therefore, if the central bank's operating costs are high which are more likely in an environment where central bank is required to intervene more, it may even incur losses on account of seigniorage revenue foregone. This may also have adverse implications for governments with chronic budget deficits as they would be deprived of the transfer of surplus to its treasury from the profitable central bank.

A distinguishing characteristic of e-money is that unlike

innovations in other retail payments media—which facilitate more efficient access to traditional form of central bank money—e-money could have the potential to become an independent medium of exchange. In that eventuality, two extreme views are being offered. On the one hand, one group perceives that in a highly technologically-advanced networked world, private entities may not require central bank money for settlement and, therefore, there may not be any central bank in future. Some of them also question whether private money is more efficient than central bank money from social welfare viewpoint and if so under what circumstance private money can replace central bank money altogether. On the other hand, there is another group of academicians and practitioners who strongly believe that central banks would continue to be as effective as ever though they may be required to respond differently in the changed environment.

8.1.4 E-money in India: In India, where cash transactions are high in number, the use of e-money can be beneficial in terms of reduced miscellaneous costs, viz. cost of printing and minting of smaller denomination notes and coins and transportation and storage costs. However, certain additional costs for setting up of network infrastructure to operate nationwide are also associated with it. The RBI has been partnering a multi-application smart card project, under the aegis of the Ministry of Communications and Information Technology, Government of India, to run a pilot project on the use of multi-application smart cards in the country. Various issues relating to technology, security, regulatory and supervisory concerns and legal implications have been examined to make the use of smart cards a viable proposition after the conclusion of the pilot project. The project is aimed at combining applications relating to banking, insurance, postal services, identification, etc. in a single card.

The Reserve Bank of India had constituted a Working Group on Electronic Money (Chairman: Zaire J. Camas) in January 2002 which submitted its Report in July 2002. The

Group identified certain areas of concern from the point of view of the central bank in the context of more widespread use of e-money. Some of the suggestions made by the Group included: (a) multi-purpose e-money to be issued only by authorised banks on a credit basis which should be strictly regulated and closely monitored, (b) redeemability should be ensured in order to preserve the unit of account function of money as well as to control money supply in the economy, and (c) reporting of e-money statistics should be ensured for the purposes of monetary policy and protection against criminal abuse such as money laundering.

8.2 E-money and Digital Money

Digital money (or *digital currency*) can be defined as an internet-based form of currency or medium of exchange which is distinct from physical currency (bank notes and coins), but allows for instantaneous transactions and borderless transfer-of-ownership. Both virtual currencies and crypto_currencies are types of digital currencies, but the converse is incorrect. Like traditional money these currencies may be used to buy physical goods and services but could also be restricted to certain communities such as for example for use inside an on-line game or social network.

According to the Bank for International Settlements', "Digital Currencies" report of November 2015, digital currency is an asset represented in digital form and having some monetary characteristics. Digital currency can be denominated to a sovereign currency and issued by the issuer responsible to redeem digital money for cash. In that case, digital currency represents electronic money (e-money). Digital currency denominated in its own units of value or with decentralized or automatic issuance will be considered as a virtual currency.

Most of the traditional money supply is bank money held on computers. This is also considered digital currency. One could argue that our increasingly cashless society means that all currencies are becoming digital (sometimes referred to as *electronic money*), but they are not presented to us as such.

8.2.1 Types of Digital Currency:

A. Virtual Currency: According to the European Central Banks', "Virtual Currency Schemes: A Further Analysis" report of February 2015, virtual currency is a digital representation of value, not issued by a central bank, credit institution or e-money institution, which, in some circumstances, can be used as an alternative to money. In the previous report of October 2012, the virtual currency was defined as a type of unregulated, digital money, which is issued and usually controlled by its developers, and used and accepted among the members of a specific virtual community.

The US Department of Treasury in 2013 defined virtual currency more tersely as "a medium of exchange that operates like a currency in some environments, but does not have all the attributes of real currency". According to these definitions, virtual currency does not have the status of a legal tender.

B. Crypto Currency: A crypto currency is a type of digital token that relies on cryptography for chaining together digital signatures of token transfers, peer-to-peer networking and decentralization. In some cases, a proof-of-work scheme is used to create and manage the currency.

For more on crypto currency, see chapter 13 of this book.

8.3 Electronic Commerce (E-commerce)

8.3.1 Types and Categories of E-commerce: E-commerce involves individuals and business organizations exchanging business information and instructions over electronic media using computers, telephones and other telecommunication equipments. Such form of doing business has been in existence ever since electronic mode of data/information exchange was developed, but its scope was limited only as a medium of exchange of information between entities with a pre-established contractual relationship. However, internet has changed the approach to e-commerce; it is no longer the same business with an additional channel for information exchange, but one with new strategy and models.

A business model generally focuses on: (a) where the business operates, i.e. the market, the competitors and the customers, (b) what it sells, i.e. its products and services, (c) the channels of distribution, i.e. the medium for sale and distribution of its products, and (d) the sources of revenue and expenditure and how these are affected. Internet has influenced all the four components of business model and thus has come to influence the business strategy in a profound way. The size of the market has grown enormously as one can access the products and services from any part of the world. So does the potential competition. The methods of reaching out to customers, receiving the response and offering services have a new, simpler and efficient alternative now, i.e. internet. The cost of advertisement, offer and delivery of services through internet has reduced considerably, forcing most companies to rework their strategies to remain in competition.

There are two types of e-commerce ventures in operation: (a) the old brick and mortar companies, who have adopted electronic medium, particularly internet, to enhance their existing products and services, and/or to offer new products and services, and (b) the pure e-ventures who have no visible physical presence. This difference has wider ramifications than mere visibility when it comes to issues like customer's trust, brand equity, ability to service the customers, adopting new business culture and cost.

Another way of classifying e-commerce is by the targeted counterpart of a business, viz. whether the counterpart is a final consumer or another business in the distribution chain. Accordingly, the two broad categories are: business-to-consumer (B2C) and business-to-business (B2B).

8.3.2 Business-to-Consumers (B2C): In the B2C category are included single e-shops, shopping malls, e-broking, e-auction, e-banking, service providers like travel related services, financial services, education, entertainment and any other form of business targeted at the final consumer. Some of the features, opportunities and concerns common to this category of business irrespective of the business segment, are the following.

Internet provides an ever growing market both in terms of number of potential customers and geographical reach. Technological development has made access to internet both cheaper and faster. More and more people across the globe are accessing the net either through PCs or other devices. The purchasing power and need for quality service of this segment of consumers are considerable. Anybody accessing Internet is a potential customer irrespective of his or her location. Thus, any business targeting final consumers cannot ignore the business potential of Internet.

Internet offers a unique opportunity to register business presence in a global market. Its effectiveness in disseminating information about one's business at a relatively cost effective manner is tremendous. Time sensitive information can be updated faster than any other media. A properly designed website can convey a more accurate and focussed image of a product or service than any other media. Use of multimedia capabilities, i.e. sound, picture, movies etc. has made internet as an ideal medium for information dissemination. However, help of other media is necessary to draw the potential customers to the web site.

The quality of service is a key feature of any e-commerce venture. The ability to sell one's product at anytime and anywhere to the satisfaction of customers is essential for e-business to succeed. Internet offers such opportunity, since the business presence is not restricted by time zone and geographical limitations. Replying to customers' queries through e-mail, offering interactive help line, accepting customers' complaints online 24 hours a day and attending to the same etc. are some of the features of e-business which enhance the quality of service to the customers. It is of crucial importance for an e-venture to realize that just as it is easier to approach a customer through internet, it is equally easy to lose him. The customer has the same facility to move over to another site.

Cost is an important issue in an e-venture. It is generally accepted that the cost of overhead, servicing and distribution etc. through internet is less compared to the traditional way of doing business. Although the magnitude of difference varies depending on the type of business and the estimates made, but there is unanimity that internet provides a substantial cost advantage and this, in fact, is one of the major driving forces for more number of traditional business adopting to e-commerce and pure e-commerce firms to sprout.

Cost of communication through www is the least compared to any other medium. Many a time one's presence in the web may bring in international enquiries, which the business might not have targeted. The business should have proper plans to address such opportunities.

There are various obstacles, which an e-commerce venture needs to overcome. Trust of customers in a web venture is an important concern. Many customers hesitate to deal with a web venture as they are not sure of the type of products and services they will receive. This is particularly true in a B2C venture like e-shop, e-mall or e-auction site. Traditional business with well-established brands and goodwill and having a physical presence face less resistance from customers in this regard than a pure e-venture.

Many B2C ventures have ultimately to deliver a product or service in physical form to the customer for a deal contracted through internet. This needs proper logistics, an efficient distribution network, and control over quality of product or service delivered. These issues are not technology related and any let off in this area can drive the customer away to the competitor or from e-commerce.

The privacy of information on the customer's preferences, credit card and bank account details etc. and customers' faith in a system where such privacy is stated to be ensured are important issues to be addressed. These are mainly technological issues, but human factor is important both at the business and at the customers' end and also in building the trust in the system.

Security of a transaction, authenticity of a deal, identification of a customer etc. are important technological and systems issues, which are major sources of concern to e-commerce. Equally important are questions of repudiation of a deal, applicability of law, jurisdiction of tax laws etc. These are important to all forms of e-commerce, whether B2C or B2B and all segments of business, i.e. manufacturing, services and finance.

Accessibility to Internet by the consumers is an important issue in B2C domain. This is particularly so in countries like India where penetration of PCs and other devices to households for access to Internet is minimal. Also important are availability of bandwidth and other infrastructure for faster and easier access. Considering that e-commerce aims at global market, deficiencies of these kinds in the developing world are no longer concerns confined to these areas, but are global e-commerce concerns.

8.3.3 Business to Business (B2B): As opposed to B2C e-commerce, in B2B domain, the parties to a deal are at different points of the product supply chain. In a B2B type domain, a company, its suppliers, dealers and bankers are networked to finalize and settle all aspects of a deal online. Perhaps, only the goods in different stages of processing physically move from the supplier to the dealer. This scenario can be extended to include the shipper, providers of different ancillary services, IT service provider and the payment system gateway etc. depending on the degree of sophistication of the available systems.

Another important feature of a B2B domain, as distinct from B2C, is that business information/data is integrated to the back office systems of parties to a deal and the state of straight through processing (STP) or near STP is achieved. This is a very significant aspect of B2B model of e-commerce, which results in improved profits through lowering cost and reducing inventories.

For example, in a B2B environment, the back office system of a company controls inventory requirement with reference to the order book position updated regularly on the basis of orders received from dealers through internet. At the optimum level of inventory, it raises a purchase order with the supplier, whose system, in turn, processes the order and confirms supply. Buyer company's system issues debit instructions on its bank account for payment to the supplier. The buyer's bank credits seller's bank with the cost of sale though a payment gateway. Similar series of transaction processes are also initiated between the company and its dealers and their respective banks. Once e-commerce relationship is established between the firms, the transactions of the type shown above can be processed with minimal human intervention and on 24 hours a day and 7 days a week basis.

New business models are emerging in B2B domain. There are portals which offer a meeting ground to buyers and sellers of different products in supply chain, more like a buyer-seller meet in international business. This has enabled relatively smaller companies to enter the global market. Banks in the portal offer financial services for deals settled through the portal.

Technology and networking are important constituents of a B2B type of business domain. Earlier, only large firms could have access to such technology and they used private networks with interface to each other for information flow and transaction processing. A major concern used to be compatibility of EDI platforms across different B2B partners. Internet with www and other standard technology have offered opportunity to relatively smaller and medium sized firms to integrate their operations in B2B model and take advantage of the benefits it offers. It has also led to standardization of software platforms.

Other new forms of business models in B2B domain are application service providers (ASPs) and service integrators. ASPs offer application software online to e-commerce companies who pay for the same according to the use without owning it. Often entire back office processing is taken care of by ASPs and other service integrators. However, the utility of such service providers will to a large extent depend on the business strategy of the e-venture.

The concerns of B2B e-commerce are similar to those of

B2C, discussed earlier. The security issues are more pronounced because of high value transfers taking place through the net. So also are the issues relating to privacy of information, law, tax repudiation etc. The other issues of importance to a B2B firm are the choice of appropriate technology, the issue of building or outsourcing, maintenance and training of personnel etc., since they involve large investments and are critical to success.

8.4 Internet Marketing

New forms of marketing also use the internet and are therefore called *internet marketing* or more generally *e-marketing*, *online marketing*, *digital marketing*. Internet marketing is sometimes considered to be broad in scope, because it not only refers to marketing on the internet, but also includes marketing done via email, wireless media as well as driving audience from traditional marketing methods like radio and billboard to internet properties or landing page.

E-marketing (electronic marketing) can be described as the marketing of the company's products that occurs over the internet and mobile. The objective behind performing electronic marketing is to increase the awareness of a particular company amongst the consumer market. E-marketing is a novel form of marketing which has been developed in conjunction with the ever growing popularity of the internet and website marketing. Being a relatively new form of marketing in India, majority of corporations continue to market themselves with use of the traditional methods of print magazine advertisements and television commercials.

Many companies, who are experts in website marketing and have been conducting business operations over the internet for a couple of years, are aware of electronic marketing and the amazing results in business success it can quickly and effortlessly achieve for them.

The growth of the internet during the past few years is undoubtedly the most important development in the history of commerce which shows no signs of abating in the future. Since the Industrial Revolution of the 19th century, no development has so dramatically altered human behaviour as the emergence of internet. Marketing has also been immensely influenced by the internet. Marketers have got a new medium for communicating and building long-term relationship with their customers at a fraction of cost they used to incur earlier. Various marketing activities can be performed more efficiently, effectively and smoothly than ever before with the help of internet. However, it is difficult to assess the potential of internet for business and foresee the probable threats brought by the new medium.

In India, the internet became available to the general public and the business in 1995. People have been mesmerized by the prowess of the internet, both as a communication tool and as an entertainment medium. The Indian corporate world was quick to realise the commercial potential of the web and embraced it as part of its business and marketing strategies. The Indian Government has also been providing the necessary infrastructural support for the internet. Worldwide, and in India also, empirical studies are being conducted to explore the possibilities of doing business on the internet, including growth in the volume of e-commerce, use of websites, on-line pricing and online advertising. However, what marketers in India think about the internet as a marketing tool and how they can use it for marketing purposes has not been attempted in a systematic manner.

9

Internet Banking and Mobile Banking

Digital technology has transformed the functioning of businesses, the world over. It has: (a) bridged the gaps in terms of the reach and the coverage of systems (b) enabled better decision-making based on latest and accurate information, (c) reduced costs and (d) improved overall improvement in efficiency. In the Indian context, the financial sector, especially the banking sector, has been a major beneficiary from the inroads made by IT.

Many new processes, products and services offered by banks and other financial intermediaries are now IT-centred. Banks have traditionally been in the forefront of harnessing technology to improve their products, services and efficiency. They have, over a long time, been using electronic and telecommunication networks for delivering a wide range of value added products and services. The delivery channels include, inter alia, direct dial-up connections, private networks, public networks and the devices including telephone, personal computers (PCs), automated teller machines (ATMs), networking of ATMs in the form of shared payment networks, and core banking solutions.

With the popularity of PCs, easy access to internet and world wide web (www), internet is increasingly used by banks as a channel for receiving instructions and delivering their products and services to their customers. This form of banking is generally referred to as internet banking, although the range of products and services offered by different banks vary widely both in their content and sophistication.

9.1 Internet Banking

9.1.1 Internet Banking and Electronic Banking (E-banking): E-banking is a generic term encompassing internet banking, telephone banking, mobile banking etc. In other words, it is a process of delivery of banking services and products through electronic channels such as satellite, telephone, internet, cell phone etc. The concept and scope of e-banking is still evolving. Internet banking is a major component of e-banking.

Internet banking offers different online services like balance enquiry, requests for cheque books, recording stop-payment instructions, balance transfer instructions, account opening and other forms of traditional banking services. These are mostly traditional services offered through internet as a new delivery channel. Banks are also offering payment services on behalf of their customers who shop in different e-shops, e-malls etc.

9.1.2 Levels of Banking Services Offered through Internet: Internet banking applications run on diverse platforms and operating systems and use different architectures. The product may support centralized (bank-wide) operations or branch level automation. It may have a distributed, client server or three-tier architecture based on a file system. Moreover, the product may run on computer systems of various types ranging from PCs, open (Unix based) systems, to proprietary main frames. These products allow different levels of access to the customers and different range of facilities. The products accessible through Internet can be classified into three types based on the levels of access granted.

A. Basic Level Services (or Information Only Systems): These refer to websites of banks which disseminate information on different products and services offered to customers and members of public in general. A bank may receive and reply to queries of customers through e-mail. General purpose information like interest rates, branch locations, product features, loan and deposit calculators are provided on the website of a bank. The sites also allow downloading of application forms. Interactivity is limited to a simple form of e-mail. No identification or authentication of customers is done and there is no interaction between the bank's production system (where current data of accounts are kept and transactions are processed) and the customer.

B. Simple Transactional Systems: These allow customers to submit their instructions, applications for different services, queries on their account balances etc., but do not permit any fund-based transactions on their accounts. These systems provide customer-specific information in the form of account balances, transaction details, statement of account etc. The information is still largely *read only*. Identification and authentication of customer takes place using relatively simple techniques (like passwords). Information is fetched from the production system of the bank in either the batch mode or offline. Thus, the main application system of the bank is not directly accessed.

C. Fully Transactional Websites: These websites allow the customers to operate on their accounts for transfer of funds, payment of different bills, subscribing to other products of the bank and to transact purchase and sale of securities etc. These systems provide bi-directional transaction capabilities. The bank allows customers to submit transactions on its systems and these directly update customers' accounts. Therefore, security and control system need to be strongest here.

The above forms of internet banking services are offered by traditional banks as an additional method of serving the customer or by new banks who deliver banking services primarily through internet or other electronic delivery channels as the value added services. Some of these banks are known as *virtual banks* or *internet-only-banks* (IOBs) and may not have any physical presence in a country despite offering different banking services. Thus, internet banking is nothing more than traditional banking services delivered through an electronic communication backbone, viz. internet. However, in the process it has thrown open issues which have ramifications beyond what a new delivery channel would normally envisage. Hence, it has compelled regulators world over to take note of this emerging channel.

9.1.3 Security Risks: Security in internet banking comprises both the computer and communication security. The aim of computer security is to preserve computing resources against abuse and unauthorized use, and to protect data from accidental and deliberate damage, disclosure and modification. The communication security aims to protect data during the transmission in computer network and distributed system.

External threats such as *hacking* [1], *sniffing* [2], *spoofing* [3] and *denial of service* [4] attacks expose banks to new security risks. Open electronic delivery channels create new security issues for banks with respect to confidentiality and integrity of information, non-repudiation of transactions, authentication of users and access control.

When a bank's system is connected to the internet, an attack could originate at any time from anywhere. Some acceptable level of security must be established before business on the internet can be reliably conducted. Following are some familiar forms of attacks:

1. An intruder gains unauthorized access and nothing more.
2. An intruder gains access and destroys, corrupts or otherwise alters data.
3. An intruder gains access and seizes control partly or wholly, perhaps denying access to privileged users.
4. An intruder does not gain access, but instead forges messages from your system.
5. An intruder does not gain access, but instead implements malicious procedures that cause the network to fail, reboot, and hang.

Modern security techniques have made cracking very difficult but not impossible. Furthermore, if the system is not configured properly or the updated patches are not installed then hackers may crack the system using security hole. A wide range of information regarding security hole and their fixes is freely available on the internet. System administrators should keep themselves updated with this information.

Most banks appear to be sensitive to external security threats. Among the issues identified for immediate attention is the development of more robust tools to verify the identity and authenticity of larger value transaction requests. [5] In addition, the banking industry needs to continue to work towards international best practices for encryption requirements, including the legality of electronic signature and records. Moreover, since many banks' internal networks rely on security technology similar to that used to manage their external systems, it is important that bankers also be sensitive to managing the security risk arising from their internal networks. If not managed properly, internal security exposures can also compromise the integrity and confidentiality of bank records and customer data. [6]

9.1.4 Internet Banking in India: Internet banking—both as a medium of delivery of banking services and as a strategic tool for business development—has gained wide acceptance internationally and is fast catching up in India with more and more banks entering the fray. India can be said to be on the threshold of a major banking revolution with net banking having already been unveiled.

The growth potential of internet banking in India is immense. Further incentives provided by banks would dissuade customers from visiting physical branches, and thus get 'hooked' to the convenience of arm-chair banking. The facility of accessing their accounts from anywhere in the world by using a home computer with internet connection, is particularly fascinating to non-resident Indians and high net worth individuals having multiple bank accounts.

Costs of banking service through the internet form a fraction of costs through conventional methods. The cost conscious banks in the country have therefore actively considered use of internet as a channel for providing services. Fully computerized banks, with better management of their customer base are in a stronger position to cross-sell their products through this channel.

A. Products and Services Offered: Banks in India are at different stages of the web-enabled banking cycle. Initially, a bank, which is not having a website, allows its customer to communicate with it through an e-mail address; communication is limited to a small number of branches and offices which have access to this e-mail account. As yet, many scheduled commercial banks in India are still in the first stage of internet banking operations.

With gradual adoption of information technology, the bank puts up a website that provides general information on the banks, its location, services available e.g. loan and deposits products, application forms for downloading and email option for enquiries and feedback. It is largely a marketing or an advertising tool. Customers are required to fill in applications on the internet and can later receive loans or other products requested for at their local branch. A few banks provide the customer to enquire into his demat account (securities/shares) holding details, transaction details and status of instructions given by him.

Some of the banks permit customers to interact with them and transact electronically with them. Such services include request for opening of accounts, requisition for cheque books, stop payment of cheques, viewing and printing statements of accounts, movement of funds between accounts within the same bank, querying on status of requests, instructions for opening of letters of credit and bank guarantees etc.

Banks are thus looking to position themselves as one-stop financial shops. Some banks have tied up with computer training companies, computer manufacturers, internet services providers and portals for expanding their internet banking services, and widening their customer base. Setting up of internet kiosks and permeation through the cable television route to widen customer base are other priority areas in the agendas of the more aggressive players.

Banks providing internet banking services have been entering into agreements with their customers setting out the terms and conditions of the services. The terms and conditions include information on the access through user-id and secret password, minimum balance and charges, authority to the bank for carrying out transactions performed through the service, liability of the user and the bank, disclosure of personal information for statistical analysis and credit scoring also, non-transferability of the facility, notices and termination etc.

The race for market supremacy is compelling banks in India to adopt the latest technology on the internet in a bid to capture new markets and customers. Under mobile banking services, customers can scan their accounts to seek balance and payments status or instruct banks to issue cheques, pay bills or deliver statements of accounts.

Compared to banks abroad, Indian banks offering online services still have a long way to go. For online banking to reach a critical mass, there has to be sufficient number of users and the sufficient infrastructure in place. Though various security options like line encryption, branch connection encryption, firewalls, digital certificates, automatic sign-offs, random pop-ups and disaster recovery sites are in place or are being looked at, there is as yet no certification authority in India offering public key infrastructure which is absolutely necessary for online banking. The customer can only be assured of a secured conduit for its online activities if an authority certifying digital signatures is in place. The communication bandwidth presently available in India is also not enough to meet the needs of high priority services like online banking and trading. Banks offering online facilities need to have an effective disaster recovery plan along with comprehensive risk management measures. Banks offering online facilities also need to calculate their downtime losses, because even a few minutes of downtime in a week could mean substantial losses.

Some banks even today do not have uninterrupted power supply unit or systems to take care of prolonged power breakdown. Proper encryption of data and effective use of passwords are also matters that leave a lot to be desired. Systems and processes have to be put in place to ensure that errors do not take place.

Users of internet banking services are required to fill up the application forms online and send a copy of the same by mail or fax to the bank. A contractual agreement is entered into by the customer with the bank for using the internet banking services. In this way, personal data in the applications forms is being held by the bank providing the service. The contract details are often one-sided, with the bank having the absolute discretion to amend or supplement any of the terms at any time. For these reasons domestic customers for whom other access points such as ATMs, telebanking, personal contact etc. are available, are often hesitant to use the internet banking services offered by Indian banks. Internet banking, as an additional delivery channel, may, therefore, be attractive and appealing as a value added service to domestic customers. Non-resident Indians for whom it is expensive and time consuming to access their bank accounts maintained in India find net banking very convenient and useful.

B. Information Technology Act, 2000: Government of India enacted The Information Technology Act, 2000, in order to provide legal recognition for transactions carried out by means of electronic data interchange and other means of electronic communication, commonly referred to as *electronic commerce*. The Act came into force with effect from October 17, 2000. The Act has also amended certain provisions of the Indian Penal Code, the Indian Evidence Act, 1872, The Bankers Book of Evidence Act, 1891 and Reserve Bank of India Act, 1934 in order to facilitate e-commerce in India. However, this Act does not apply to:

1. A negotiable instrument as defined in Section 13 of the Negotiable Instruments Act, 1881.
2. A power of attorney as defined in Section 1A of the Power of Attorney Act, 1882.
3. A trust as defined in Section 3 of the Indian Trusts Act, 1882.
4. A will as defined in clause (h) of Section 2 of the Indian Succession Act, 1925.
5. Any contract for the sale or conveyance of immovable property or any interest in such property.

6. Any such class of documents or transactions as may be notified by the Central Government in the official Gazette.

Section 72 of the Information Technology Act, 2000, casts an obligation of confidentiality against disclosure of any electronic record, register, correspondence and information, except for certain purposes and violation of this provision is a criminal offence.

In the course of providing internet banking services the banks in India are facing new challenges relating to online opening of accounts, authentication, secrecy of customers accounts, non-repudiation, liability standards and consumer protection etc.

9.2 Mobile Banking

9.2.1 Introduction: Developments in mobile telephony, as also the mobile phone density in the India, present a unique opportunity to leverage the mobile platform to meet the objectives and challenges of financial inclusion. By harnessing the potential of mobile technology, large sections of the un-banked and under-banked society can be empowered to become inclusive through the use of electronic banking services.

The Payment and Settlement Systems (PSS) Act, 2007 empowers the RBI to authorize and regulate entities operating payment systems in the country. RBI has, over a period of time, placed importance on the move towards electronic payments and thereby a *less-cash* society. Towards this end, the RBI has been promoting and nurturing the growth of various modes of electronic payments including the pre-paid payment instruments, card payments, mobile banking etc.

The Payment Systems Vision Document 2012-15 of RBI, reflects the commitment towards provision of safe, efficient, accessible, inclusive, interoperable and authorised payment and settlement systems in the country. Recent experience shows that the share of paper-based instruments in the volume of total non-cash transactions has been declining in favour of electronic payments. In addition to the growth in volume as well as value processed by RTGS, the retail electronic segment too has registered a significant growth. Though overall volume of transactions in mobile banking is low, there has been significant growth in the volume recently.

9.2.2 Mobile Banking Regulatory Framework: In view of the potential of mobile as a channel for offering financial services in the country, RBI issued the first set of guidelines on mobile banking in October 2008. The mandate was that all transactions should originate from one bank account and terminate in another bank account. At this time, a few banks had already started offering information-based services like balance enquiry, stop payment instruction of cheques, transactions enquiry, location of the nearest ATM/branch etc. through this medium.

The guidelines issued by RBI in October 2008, permitted banks to facilitate funds transfer from one bank account to another bank account, both for personal remittances and purchase of goods and services. Banks were directed on the regulatory/supervisory issues, registration of customers for mobile banking, to ensure technology standards, interoperability, inter-bank clearing and settlement arrangements for fund transfers, customer grievance and redressal mechanism and transaction limits in an attempt to ensure safe, secure transfer of funds.

Under extant regulatory prescriptions, there is no monetary restriction on fund transfer effected through mobile banking as it is left to the risk perception of each bank and policies approved by their respective Boards. However, end-to-end encryption for transactions in excess of ₹ 5,000 has been mandated by RBI. Similarly, mobile as a channel for funds transfer from a bank account for cash payout to a beneficiary who does not have a bank account at ATMs/BCs—₹ 10,000 per transaction with a cap of ₹ 25,000 per beneficiary has also been permitted by RBI (under the Domestic Money Transfer Guidelines).

In line with these guidelines, banks have been offering mobile banking services to their customers through various channels such as SMS, USSD channel, mobile banking application etc. However, real time inter-bank mobile banking payments have been facilitated through the setting up of the inter-bank mobile payment services (IMPS), now termed as immediate payment service, and operated by the NPCI with the approval of RBI.

The IMPS has enhanced the efficiency of mobile banking by enabling real time transfer of funds between bank accounts and providing a centralised inter-bank settlement service for mobile banking transactions. The IMPS has also been enhanced to support merchant payments using mobile phones to promote less cash society.

Under the PSS Act, RBI had given permission for mobile banking services to 201 banks as on December 31, 2016. For the month of April 2019, the value of mobile banking transactions stood at ₹ 3,966.03 billion.

9.2.3 Various Channels for Mobile Banking:

A. Mobile Banking: SMS-based Channel: SMS is a popular and widely used channel in mobile phones. It is ubiquitously available in all handsets irrespective of make and model and also GSM and CDMA enabled handsets. Most customers are very conversant with the SMS channel and use the same for various services including the short messaging. Many popular mobile VAS services such as cricket, jokes, horoscopes, etc. are based on SMS and used widely by customers.

Given the advantages offered by SMS channel, many banks have offered mobile banking services through the SMS channel. This includes non-financial services such as balance enquiry, mini statement, cheque book request, transaction alerts etc., and financial services such as funds transfer, mobile/DTH recharge, bill payments etc.

B. Mobile Banking: USSD-based Channel: Unstructured supplementary service data (USSD) is a protocol used by GSM cellular telephones to communicate with the telecom service provider's systems. USSD can be used for WAP browsing, pre-paid callback service, mobile-money services, location-based content services, menu-based information services, and as part of configuring the phone on the network.

USSD messages are up to 182 alphanumeric characters in length. Unlike short message service (SMS) messages, USSD messages create a real-time connection during a USSD session. The connection remains open, allowing a two-way exchange of a sequence of data. This makes USSD more interactive and advantageous than services that use SMS.

USSD platform which is MNO dependent can be efficiently used by the mobile banking platforms. Realizing the benefits and potential of USSD-based mobile banking, some of the banks have launched USSD-based mobile banking services, e.g. State Bank of India, Canara Bank, ICICI Bank, with the help of telecom aggregators who in turn have tied up with few MNOs. For instance, ICICI Bank has tied up with Idea, Aircel, Tata Docomo, Reliance and MTNL for offering USSD platform to its customers on their GSM network.

C. Mobile Banking: Application-based: All banks who have received the approval from RBI for mobile banking are offering the application-based mobile banking channel to their customers. Customers can download the mobile banking application and perform variety of services including the following: (a) Non-financial transactions such as balance enquiry, mini statement, cheque book request, (b) financial transactions such as funds transfer, mobile/DTH recharge, bill payments etc.

The mobile application is offered on various platforms such as Java, Symbian, Blackberry OS, Windows, Android, Apple iOS etc. Many Banks have made the mobile application available in the app stores such as Google, Apple, Blackberry, etc. for easy search and download by the customers.

Following are the advantages of the application-based mobile banking:

- Applications once downloaded are easy to use for the customers who are proficient in using the smart phone based applications.
- Banks have made these applications compliant with most of the latest operating systems covering the large range of smart

phones in use.

- It has been experienced by the banks that once customer has used the application-based mobile banking, he continues to use the same unless there is a change of the handset and/or mobile number.
- The application-based mobile banking can also communicate using SMS and GPRS (data) channels with the mobile banking system of the bank.

9.2.4 Challenges Faced by Banks: Despite the potential for mobile banking and the regulatory provisions enabling greater use of mobiles as a channel for financial services in general, and for financial inclusion in particular, banks are facing some challenges in taking mobile banking to the desired level. These challenges are essentially in two fronts:

1. Customer enrolment related issues.
2. Technical issues.

A. Customer Enrolment Related Issues: These are as under:

1. Mobile number registration.
2. M-PIN generation process.
3. Concerns relating to security are a factor affecting on-boarding of customers.
4. Bank staff education.
5. Customer education.

(a) Mobile Number Registration: For a customer, in order to conduct a mobile payment transaction, his/her mobile number needs to be registered with the bank. The process for mobile number registration is implemented differently across banks. Currently, the process for mobile number registration involves the following:

- Customer mandatorily needs to go to the bank branch for most of the banks to register his number and fill in the application form (paper-based). After verification, his number gets registered in the CBS and in the bank's mobile banking system.
- Some leading banks have provided the facility for customer to register mobile number at their bank's ATMs

using 2FA authentication of ATM card + ATM PIN.

In both the above cases, the customer needs to physically go to the branch/ATM in order to register their mobile number, which acts as a barrier in many cases, besides delaying the entire process. Further, even where the above process of registration through ATMs is provided, it is restricted to the use of own-bank ATMs and the same is not possible at present by going to any other bank ATMs. The process for mobile number registration needs to be simpler for customer to get on-boarded.

(b) M-PIN Generation: M-PIN is the second factor of authentication that customer needs to use in order to conduct mobile banking transaction. Customer needs M-PIN from his respective bank in order to get started with mobile payments. Currently, the process for M-PIN generation is implemented differently across banks, and involves the following:

- For most banks, after the mobile number registration at branch/any bank ATM, customer receives M-PIN via SMS on their registered mobile number. In certain cases, customer receives the M-PIN through postal mail.
- Some leading banks have provided the facility for generating and changing M-PIN from the handset itself using the mobile banking application and providing the authentication parameters as required by the bank (e.g. debit card details such as debit card number, ATM PIN, and expiry date). These inputs are captured and sent through registered mobile number, for the purpose of M-PIN generation.
- Some leading banks have also provided the facility to generate and change M-PIN through alternate channels such as IVR, ATM, and internet banking. Customer may be able to make merchant payment using just his mobile number and M-PIN/OTP (one-time password) on the merchant interface. The M-PIN can be only interfaced on acquiring bank's interface such as USSD, application etc. for security reasons. The merchant based interfaces can accept OTP for authentication.

(c) Concerns Related to Security: One of the major

factors affecting customer on-boarding and usage of mobile banking services is the concern relating to security of transactions effected using the mobile phone. While mobile banking application is an end-to-end encrypted channel, the other access channels viz. SMS, USSD, IVR, are not end-to-end encrypted. However, in order to enjoy the higher level of security available in the application-based mobile banking, the customer's handset has to be GPRS-enabled.

Since SMS facility is available on all handsets, the issue of security can be addressed if the SMS can be encrypted end-to-end, thus allaying any concerns relating to lack of security in this channel.

In addition to this, another important aspect adding to the concerns on the part of customers relate to how their complaints and grievances will be addressed for transacting on this channel—whether through their bank or through their mobile service provider.

(d) Bank Staff Training: For effective and efficient implementation of providing mobile banking facilities to the customers it is imperative that the banks staff is well-versed and thoroughly trained in various aspects of the mobile banking.

(e) Customer Education: Banks must continue to invest in handholding and educating customers to increase the awareness of various aspects of mobile banking. Banks collectively may invest in marketing and advertising for widespread promotion of mobile banking.

B. Technical Issues: Technical aspects which are posing a challenge relate to the following:

1. Access channels for transactions.
2. Cumbersome transaction process.
3. Co-ordination with MNOs in mobile banking eco-system.

(a) Access Channels for Transaction: Once the customer mobile number is registered and M-PIN is generated, customer may use any of the access channels provided by the bank for conducting mobile banking transactions. Currently, while most banks have provided mobile banking application and SMS facility as access channels, a few banks have also provided other access channels such as USSD, WAP, IVR, etc. Some banks also provide a combination of a few of these channels (application + SMS, application + USSD) for better security.

(b) Cumbersome Transaction Process: In the present scenario, with various banks offering various channels for their customers to undertake mobile banking transactions, the user experience is certainly not uniform across banks/channels. The customer is required to provide different set of inputs (authentication parameters) for each type of access channel, thus making the entire transaction process cumbersome.

(c) Co-ordination with MNOs in Mobile Banking Eco-system: In order to offer a more secure and better user experience to their customers through their mobile banking channels, banks need a greater level of coordination with the telecom service providers.

Endnotes

1. Hacking refers to the practice of breaking into a computer without authorisation, for malicious reasons, just to prove it can be done, or for other personal reasons.
2. Sniffing involves the use of a software program that is illicitly inserted somewhere on a network to capture ("sniff") user passwords as they pass through the system.
3. Spoofing refers to an attempt to gain access to a system by posing as an authorised user.
4. A denial of service attack represents an attempt to overwhelm a server with requests so that it cannot respond to legitimate traffic.
5. Identification is concerned with positively establishing the identity of the person or organisation conducting the transaction. Passwords are a common approach although evolving approaches such as biometrics may become increasingly prevalent. Authorisation is concerned with establishing the authority that an individual has to conduct a particular transaction.
6. Attacks on internal systems including those by employees are more frequent than external attacks in many organisations.

10

E-payment of Taxes

10.1 Payment of Income Tax

Central Board of Direct Taxes (CBDT), New Delhi, is part of the Department of Revenue in the Ministry of Finance. While the CBDT provides essential inputs for policy and planning of direct taxes in India, it is also responsible for administration of direct tax laws through its Income Tax Department.

The Income Tax Department has taken several initiatives in recent years to promote the use of information technology (IT) and IT-enabled services for efficient and transparent administration of income tax.

E-payment facility is provided to the taxpayers for making income tax payment through internet banking facility or through internet by using credit/debit cards.

E-payment of tax is mandatory in certain cases. Thus, all companies and assesses required to get their accounts audited under Section 44AB of the Income Tax Act, 1961 are mandatorily required to make e-payment of tax. Other assesses may also make payment of tax electronically.

E-payment of tax can be made only through a bank which provides e-payment facility. Some of the banks are providing facility of opening a separate *e-payment of taxes account* in addition to the normal bank account.

An assessee can make payment from his own account or from the account of any other person in an authorized bank. However, the *challan* must clearly indicate the permanent account number (PAN) of the assessee on whose behalf the payment if made

Similarly, there is facility of e-filing of returns. E-filing of income tax return is the process of electronically filing returns through internet which can be filed at any time at any place.

Likewise, digital signature facility is also available. A person desiring to furnish his return of income electronically, may sign it digitally or manually. For signing the return digitally, he is required to obtain a digital signature. A digital signature is the electronic signature issued by the certifying authority that shows the authenticity of the person signing the same.

10.2 Payment of Goods and Services Tax (GST)

GST became operative on July 1, 2017. GST is a tax on goods and services with comprehensive and continuous chain of set-off benefits up to the retailer level. It is essentially a tax only on value addition at each stage, and a supplier at each stage is permitted to set-off, through a tax credit mechanism, the GST paid on the purchase of goods and services. Ultimately, the burden of GST is borne by the end-user (i.e. final consumer) of the commodity/service.

Every registered person is required to compute his tax liability on a monthly basis by setting off the input tax credit against the outward tax liability. If there is any balance tax liability, the same is required to be paid to the government.

There are 3 ledgers prescribed by the government which are required to be maintained by every taxpayer.

- **Electronic Tax Liability Register:** It shows the total tax liability of a registered person at any point of time.
- **Electronic Cash Ledger:** It displays the total amount deposited by the taxpayer towards discharge of his tax liability.
- **Electronic Credit Ledger:** It records all the taxes paid on the inputs.

Under the GST regime, for any intra-state supply, taxes to be paid are the CGST, going into the account of the Central Government and the SGST, going into the account of the concerned State Government. For any inter-state supply, tax to be paid is IGST which will have components of both CGST and SGST. In addition, certain categories of registered persons—(e.g. e-commerce operators responsible for tax collection at source (TCS) and government departments responsible for tax deduction at source (TDS)—are required to pay TCS and TDS to the government account.

In addition, wherever applicable, interest, penalty, fees and any other payment will also be required to be made.

In general, the supplier of goods and/or service is liable to pay GST. However in specified cases like imports and other notified supplies, the liability may be cast on the recipient under the reverse charge mechanism.

GST payment is to be made by the taxable person at the time of supply of goods and at the time of supply of services. The time is generally the earliest of one of the three events, namely receiving payment, issuance of invoice or completion of supply. Different situations envisaged and different tax points have been explained in the GST law.

Liability to pay tax arises when the taxable person crosses the threshold limit of turnover, i.e. ₹ 20 lakh (₹ 10 lakh for Special Category States) except in certain specified cases where the taxable person is liable to pay GST even though he has not crossed the threshold limit.

10.2.1 Features of GST Payment: The payment processes under GST regime have the following features:

1. Electronically-generated challan from GSTN Common Portal in all modes of payment and no use of manually prepared challan.
2. Hassle free, anytime, anywhere mode of payment of tax.
3. Convenience of making payment online.
4. Logical tax collection data in electronic format.
5. Faster remittance of tax revenue to the government account.
6. Paperless transactions.
7. Speedy accounting and reporting.
8. Electronic reconciliation of all receipts.
9. Simplified procedure for banks.
10. Warehousing of digital challan.

10.2.2 Methods of GST Payment: Payment of GST can be made electronically with a common *challan* (i.e. document for payment of taxes) for all the taxes. Various modes of GST payment are available to the taxpayer including the following:

1. Through debit of credit ledger of the taxpayer maintained on the common portal of GSTN. Only tax can be paid. Interest, penalty and fees cannot be paid by debit in the credit ledger. Taxpayers are allowed to take credit of taxes paid on inputs (input tax credit) and utilize the same for payment of output tax. However, no input tax credit on account of CGST shall be utilized towards payment of SGST and vice versa. The credit of IGST would be permitted to be utilized for payment of IGST, CGST and SGST in that order.
2. In cash by debit in the cash ledger of the taxpayer maintained on the common portal of GSTN. Money can be deposited in the cash ledger by different modes, namely:

- E-payment (internet banking, credit card, debit card).
- Real time gross settlement (RTGS) [1]
- National electronic funds transfer (NEFT). [2]
- Over the counter payment in branches of banks authorized to accept deposit of GST.

Timing of payment is from 00.00 hrs. till 20.00 hrs.

Endnotes

1. National Electronic Funds Transfer (NEFT): Electronic Funds Transfer (EFT) system was introduced in the mid-1990s. EFT facilitates transfer of funds from one bank account to another. In the beginning EFT system was permitted only for government transactions and RBI-initiated payments. NEFT is an electronic message-based payment system, and was introduced by the Reserve Bank of India in November 2005 to replace the EFT system which was public key infrastructure (PKI)-enabled and the settlements were effected on a decentralized mode.
2. Real Time Gross Settlement (RTGS) System: The Indian RTGS system was operationalised in March 2004. The system started operations with four banks and settled only inter-bank transactions. Subsequently, the system was opened for

settlement of customer transactions. It was operationalised for settlement of multilateral net settlement batch (MNSB) files from September 2006.

11

Demonetization of High Denomination Currency Notes and Digital Payments

Demonetization is the act of stripping a currency unit of its status as legal tender. Demonetization is necessary whenever there is a change of national currency. The old unit of currency must be retired and replaced with a new currency unit. The process of demonetization involves either introducing new notes or coins of the same currency or completely replacing the old currency with new currency. The opposite of demonetization is remonetization where a form of payment is restored as legal tender. There are multiple reasons why nations demonetize their local units of currency. Some reasons include combating inflation, curbing corruption, and discouraging a cash system.

11.1 Prime Minister's Historic Announcement

Various policies and programmes announced by Prime Minister Shri Narendra Modi, from time to time, have led to India emerging as a bright spot in the global economy. India is a preferred destination for investment and India is also an easier place to do business in. Leading financial agencies have shared their optimism about India's growth as well. Combined with this, Indian enterprise and innovation has received a fillip due to the *Make-in-India*, *Start-up India* and *Stand-up India* initiatives that seek to encourage enterprise, innovation and research in India. However, the problems of black money and corruption have been plaguing the economy.

A radical governance-cum-social engineering measure was enacted on November 8, 2016 when the Prime Minister announced the demonetization of two largest denomination notes—₹ 500 and ₹ 1,000—together comprising 86 percent of all the cash in circulation. These notes ceased to be legal tender with immediate effect, except for a few specified purposes (such as paying utility bills). These notes were to be deposited in the banks by December 30, 2016 while restrictions were placed on cash withdrawals. In other words, restrictions were placed on the convertibility of domestic money and bank deposits.

In terms of value, the annual report of the Reserve Bank of India (RBI) of March 31, 2016 stated that total bank notes in circulation valued to ₹ 16.42 trillion of which nearly 86 percent (around ₹ 14.18 trillion) were ₹ 500 and ₹ 1,000 banknotes.

Government also announced the issuance of new ₹ 500 and ₹ 2,000 banknotes of the Mahatma Gandhi New Series in exchange for the old banknotes. Banknotes of ₹ 100, ₹ 50, ₹ 20, ₹ 10, ₹ 5, ₹ 2 and ₹ 1 remained as legal tenders and thus unaffected by the decision of the Government.

Persons holding old notes of ₹ 500 or ₹ 1,000 were able to deposit these notes in bank or post offices from November 10, 2016 onwards till December 30, 2016. There were also some limits placed on the withdrawals of new notes from ATMs and banks.

The Government's move was aimed at eradicating counterfeit currency, fighting tax evasion, eliminating black money, curbing terrorist financing and promoting a cashless economy.

Prime Minister assured the people that these decisions would fully protect the interests of honest and hard-working citizens of India and that those ₹ 500 and ₹ 1,000 notes hoarded by anti-national and anti-social elements would become worthless pieces of paper. He reiterated that the steps taken by the Government would strengthen the hands of the common citizens in the fight against corruption, black money and counterfeit notes.

Fully sensitive to some of the difficulties the common citizens may face in the coming days, the Prime Minister announced a series of steps to help overcome the potential problems. He stated that on humanitarian grounds, ₹ 500 and ₹ 1,000 notes would be accepted at government hospitals, pharmacies in government hospitals (with prescription of a doctor), booking counters for railway tickets, government buses, airline ticket counters, petrol, diesel and gas stations of oil companies of public sector undertakings (PSUs), consumer co-operative stores authorized by the Central or State Government, milk booths authorized by State Governments, and crematoria and burial grounds.

He emphasized that there was no restriction on any kind of non-cash payments by cheques, demand drafts, debit or credit cards and electronic funds transfer.

In his address, the Prime Minister shared the insight into how the magnitude of cash in circulation was linked to inflation and how the inflation situation has worsened due to the cash deployed through corrupt means. He added that it adversely affected the poor and the neo-middle class people. He cited the example of the problems being faced by the honest citizens while buying houses.

By making the high denomination notes worthless, individuals and entities with huge sums of black money were forced to convert the money at a bank which is by law required to acquire tax information from the entity. If the entity could not provide proof of making any tax payments on the cash, a tax penalty of 200 percent of the tax owed was imposed.

After the official announcement by Prime Minister Modi, the Governor of the Reserve Bank of India, Urjit Patel, and Economic Affairs secretary, Shaktikanta Das explained at a press conference that while the supply of notes of all denominations had increased by 40 percent between 2011 and 2016, the ₹ 500 and ₹ 1,000 banknotes increased by 76 percent and 109 percent respectively during this period, owing to forgery. This forged cash was then used to fund terrorist activities against India. As a result, the decision to eliminate the notes had been taken.

Patel also informed that the decision had been made about six months ago, and the printing of new banknotes of denomination ₹ 500 and ₹ 2,000 had already started. However, only the top members of the government, security agencies and the central bank were aware of the move.

11.2 Objectives of Demonetization

These were as under:

11.2.1 Eliminating Black Money: In recent years, the issue of corruption and black money has come to the forefront after a series of financial scandals. Generation of black money—and its stashing abroad in tax havens and offshore financial centres—has dominated discussions and debates in public fora during the recent past. Members of the Parliament, the Supreme Court of India and the public at large have unequivocally expressed concern on the issue, particularly after some reports suggested enormous estimates of such unaccounted wealth being held abroad.

After uproar in the Parliament, the Government of India came out with a *White Paper* on Black Money in May 2012. The *White Paper* presented the different facets of black money and its complex relationship with policy and administrative regime in the country. It also reflected upon the policy options and strategies that the Government had been pursuing to address the issue of black money and corruption in public life.

To meet the deadline set by the Honourable Supreme Court for the previous Government, the new Government of Prime Minister Narendra Modi constituted a Special Investigation Team (SIT), soon after assuming office on May 26, 2014. Headed by Justice M.B. Shah, a former judge of the Supreme Court, SIT was notified on May 27, 2014 to look into the issue of black money.

11.2.2 Curbing Corruption: Corruption is both morally abhorrent and imposes economic costs. Corruption distorts the decision-making mechanism and leads to an inefficient distribution of resources. Improving anti-corruption efforts is one of the highest rated priorities of the Government of India.

11.2.3 Preventing Money Laundering: *Money laundering* is the process of transforming the proceeds of crime and corruption into ostensibly legitimate assets. In recent years, prevention of money laundering has assumed importance in international financial relationships. [1]

11.2.4 Eradicating Counterfeit Currency: The incidence of fake Indian currency notes in higher denomination had increased. For ordinary persons, the fake notes looked similar to genuine notes, even though no security feature had been copied. The fake notes were used for anti-national and illegal activities. High denomination notes had been misused by terrorists and for hoarding black money. In the cash-based economy of India, circulation of fake Indian currency notes was a menace.

11.2.5 Fighting Tax Evasion: Black money and tax evasion have been eating into the social and moral fabric of the Indian society. They are undermining the socio-economic objectives of national policies. They are responsible for conspicuous and wasteful consumption, reduced savings, and increasing gap between the rich and the poor. Black money in social, economic and political space of the country has a debilitating effect on the institutions of governance and conduct of public policy in the country. Governance failure adversely affects the interests of vulnerable and disadvantaged sections of the society. The success of an inclusive growth strategy critically hinges on the capacity of society to root out the evil of corruption and black money from its very foundations.

The effects of tax evasion, resulting in black money, on an economy are indeed disastrous. Tax evasion leads to the creation of black money which in turn is a menace to the economy in its own way. Tax evasion and black money encourage concentration of economic power in the hands of undesirable groups in the country.

11.2.6 Combating Terrorist Financing: India has been a victim of terrorist attacks time and again. Demonetization scheme is expected to choke funding for arms smuggling, espionage, and terrorism through *hawala* transactions. [2]

11.2.7 Promoting a Cashless Economy: The benefits of a cashless economy include: (a) reduced cash and hence more safety, (b) faster payment, (c) reduced number of visits to banks, (d) interest earning on money in the bank, (e) quick settlement of transactions, and (f) improved accounting and book-keeping.

In order to promote the above objectives, the scheme to withdraw legal tender character of old bank notes in the denominations of ₹ 500 and ₹ 1,000 was introduced. Demonetisation was aimed at signalling a regime change, emphasizing the government's determination to penalize illicit activities and the associated wealth. In effect, the tax on illicit activities as well as on legal activities that were not disclosed to the tax authorities was sought to be permanently and punitively increased.

11.3 Package for Promotion of Digital and Cashless Economy

In the aftermath of the cancellation of the legal tender character of old ₹ 500 and ₹ 1,000 notes, there has been a surge in the digital transactions through the use of credit/debit cards and mobile phone applications/e-wallets etc. To further accelerate this process, the Central Government has announced from time-to-time, various incentives and measures for the promotion of digital and cashless economy in the country. These incentives/measures have included the following:

1. The Central Government petroleum PSUs (public sector undertakings) shall give incentive by offering a discount at the rate of 0.75 percent of the sale price to consumers on purchase of petrol/diesel if payment is made through digital means.
2. To expand digital payment infrastructure in rural areas, the Central Government through NABARD will extend financial support to eligible banks for deployment of 2 PoS devices each in 1 lakh villages with a population of less than 10,000. These PoS machines are intended to be deployed at primary co-operative societies, milk societies, agricultural input dealers to facilitate agri-related transactions through digital means. This will benefit farmers of 1 lakh village covering a total population of nearly 75 crore who will have the facility to transact cashless in their villages for their agri needs.
3. The Central Government through NABARD will also support rural regional banks and co-operative banks to

issue "Rupay Kisan Cards" to 4.32 crore Kisan Credit Card holders to enable them to make digital transactions at PoS machines/micro ATMs/ATMs.

4. Railway, through its sub-urban railway network, shall provide incentive by way of discount up to 0.5 percent to customers for monthly or seasonal tickets from January 1, 2017, if payment is made through digital means.
5. All railway passengers buying online ticket shall be given free accidental insurance cover of up to ₹ 10 lakh.
6. For paid services, e.g. catering, accommodation, retiring rooms etc. being offered by the railways through its affiliated entities/corporations to the passengers, it will provide a discount of 5 percent for payment of these services through digital means. All the passengers travelling on railways availing these services may avail the benefit.
7. Public sector insurance companies will provide incentive, by way of discount or credit, up to 10 percent of the premium in general insurance policies and 8 percent in new life policies of Life Insurance Corporation sold through the customer portals, in case payment is made through digital means.
8. The Central Government departments and PSUs will ensure that transactions fee/MDR charges associated with payment through digital means shall not be passed on to the consumers and all such expenses shall be borne by them. State Governments have been advised that the State Governments and its organizations should also consider absorbing the transaction fee/MDR charges related to digital payments to them and consumers should not be asked to bear it.
9. Public sector banks are advised that merchant should not be required to pay more than ₹ 100 per month as monthly rental for PoS terminals/micro ATMs/mobile PoS from the merchants to bring small merchants on board the digital payment eco-system. Nearly 6.5 lakh machines by public sector banks have been issued to merchants who will be benefited by the lower rentals while promoting digital

transactions. With lower rentals, more merchants will install such machines and promote digital transactions.

10. No service tax will be charged on digital transaction charges/MDR for transactions up to ₹ 2,000 per transaction.
11. For the payment of toll at toll plazas on national highways using RFID card/fast tags, a discount of 10 percent will be available to users during the year 2016-17.
12. Launch of the BHIM (Bharat Interface for Money) app for smart phones. This is based on the new Unified Payments Interface (UPI) which has created inter-operability of digital transactions. As on April 30, 2019, there had been 45.96 million downloads of BHIM app. As of May 2019, 112 banks were live on BHIM and over 15.77 million transactions had been conducted.
13. Launch of BHIM USSD 2.0, a product that allows the 350 million feature phone users to take advantage of the UPI.
14. Launch of Aadhaar Merchant Pay, aimed at 350 million who do not have phones. This enables anyone with just an Aadhaar number and a bank account to make a merchant payment using his biometric identification. Aadhaar Merchant Pay will soon be integrated into BHIM and the necessary POS devices will soon be rolled out.
15. Reductions in fees (merchant discount rate) paid on digital transactions and transactions that use the UPI. There have also been relaxations of limits on the use of payment wallets. Tax benefits have also been provided for to incentivize digital transactions.
16. Encouraging the adoption of PoS devices beyond the current 1.5 million, through tariff reductions.

Endnotes

1. Prevention of Money Laundering Act (PMLA), 2002 was enacted to prevent money laundering and provide for confiscation of property derived from, or involved in, money laundering and for matters connected therewith or incidental thereto. The Act also addresses international obligations under the Political Declaration and Global Programme of Action

adopted by the General Assembly of the United Nations to prevent money laundering.

2. **Hawala Transactions:** The hawala system has existed since the 8th century between Arabic and Muslim traders alongside the Silk Road and beyond as a protection against theft. It is believed to have arisen in the financing of long-distance trade around the emerging capital trade centres in the early medieval period.

   Meaning: Hawala (reference/trust) is a popular and informal value transfer system based on the past record and honour of a huge network of money brokers—primarily located in the Middle East and the Indian subcontinent—operating outside of, or parallel to, traditional banking, financial channels, and remittance systems. Dubai has been standing out for decades as a welcoming hub for hawala transactions worldwide.

   Working Mechanism: In the most basic variant of the hawala system, money is transferred via a network of hawala brokers. It is the transfer of money without actually moving it or money transfer without money movement.

   Let us suppose a customer (named A) approaches a hawala broker (named B) in New York and gives a sum of money (US$ 1,000) that is to be transferred to a recipient (named C) in New Delhi. Along with the money, A specifies something like a password (e.g. red rose) that will lead to the money being paid out. The hawala broker B calls another hawala broker (named D) in New Delhi—the recipient's city—and informs D about the agreed password and other details regarding funds and meeting place and time. Now, the intended recipient (C)—who also has been informed by A about the password etc. approaches D and tells him the agreed password. If the password is correct, then D releases the transferred sum to C in Indian rupees (₹ 70,000 if 1 US$ = ₹ 70), usually minus a small commission. B now basically owes D the money that D had paid out to C. Thus, D has to trust B's promise to settle the debt at a later date.

   Apparently, hawala mechanism can work in the reverse also if funds are to be transferred from New Delhi to New York.

   Features: The unique feature of the system is that no promissory instruments are exchanged between the hawala brokers. The transaction takes place entirely on the trust/honour system. As the system does not depend on the legal enforceability of claims, it can operate even in the absence of a legal and juridical environment. Trust and extensive use of connections, such as family relations and regional affiliations, are the components that distinguish it from other remittance systems.

Informal records are kept of individual transactions, and a running tally of the amount owed by one broker to another is kept. Settlements of debts between hawala brokers can take a variety of forms (such as goods, services, properties etc.) and need not take the form of direct cash transactions.

In addition to commissions, hawala brokers often earn their profits through bypassing official exchange rates. Generally, the funds enter the system in the source country's currency (in this example, US$) and leave the system in the recipient country's currency (in this example, Indian rupees). As settlements often take place without any foreign exchange transactions, they can be made at other than official exchange rates.

Hawala is attractive to customers because it provides a fast and convenient transfer of funds, usually with a far lower commission than that charged by banks. Its advantages are most pronounced when the receiving country applies unprofitable exchange rate regulations or when the banking system in the receiving country is less efficient.

Hawala is often used for migrant workers' remittances to their countries of origin. Hawala route can be used to facilitate drug smuggling, money laundering, tax evasion, and anonymously movement of fund for terrorist activities. Hence, it is illegal in many countries including India.

12

Digitization and Digital India (DI): Vision 2019

12.1 Economics of Digitization

The economics of digitization is the field of economics that studies how digitization affects markets and how digital data can be used to study economics. Digitization is the process by which technology lowers the costs of storing, sharing, and analyzing data. This process has changed how consumers behave, how industrial activity is organized, and how governments operate. The economics of digitization exists as a distinct field of economics for two reasons. First, new economic models are needed because many traditional assumptions about information no longer hold in a digitized world. Second, the new types of data generated by digitization require new methods to analyze.

Research in the economics of digitization touches on several fields of economics including industrial organization, labour economics, and intellectual property. Consequently, many of the contributions to the economics of digitization have also found an intellectual home in these fields. An underlying theme in much of the work in the field is that existing government regulation of copyright, security, and anti-trust is inappropriate in the modern world. For example, information goods, such as news articles and movies, now have zero marginal cost of production and sharing. This has made the piracy of information goods common and has increased competition between providers of information goods. Research in the economics of digitization studies how policy should adapt in response to these changes.

A key issue in the economics of digitization is how much people value internet-based services. The motivation for this question is two-fold. First, economists are interested in understanding digitization related policies such as network infrastructure investment and subsidies for internet access. Second, economists want to measure the gains to consumers from the internet. This is an especially important topic because many economists believe that traditional measures of economic growth, such as GDP, understate the true benefits of improving technology.

Digitization has coincided with the increased prominence of platforms and marketplaces that connect diverse agents in social and economic activity. Platforms are most readily identified with their technical standards, i.e. engineering specifications for hardware and standards for software. The pricing and product strategies that platforms use differ from those of traditional firms because of the presence of network effects. Network effects are within platforms because participation by one group affects the utility of another group. Furthermore, network effects make the analysis of competition between platforms more complex than the analysis of competition between traditional firms. Much work in the economics of digitization studies the question of how these firms should operate and how they compete with each other. A particularly important issue is whether successful online platforms should be subject to anti-trust actions.

Digitization has partially or fully replaced many tasks that were previously done by human labourers. At the same time, computers have made some workers much more productive. Economists are interested in understanding how these two forces interact in determining labour market outcomes. For example, a large literature studies the magnitude and causes of skill-biased technical change, the process by which technology improves wages for educated workers.

Another consequence of digitization is that it has drastically reduced the costs of communication between workers across different organizations and locations. This has led to a change in the geographic and contractual organization of production.

Privacy and data security is an area where digitization has substantially changed the costs and benefits to various economic actors. Traditional policies regarding privacy circumscribed the ability of government agencies to access individual data. However, the large-scale ability of firms to collect, parse, and analyze detailed micro level data about consumers has shifted the policy focus. Now, the concern is whether access consumer data of firms should be regulated and restricted or not.

There are many other policies related to digitization that are of interest to economists. For example, digitization may affect government effectiveness and accountability. Digitization also makes it easier for firms in one jurisdiction to supply consumers in another. This creates challenges for tax enforcement. Many safety and quality enforcement regulations may no longer be necessary with the advent of online reputation systems. Lastly, digitization is of great importance to health care policy. For example, electronic medical records have the potential to make healthcare more effective but pose challenges to privacy policy.

12.2 Digital Economy and Knowledge Economy

12.2.1 Digital Economy: It refers to an economy that is based on digital technologies. The digital economy is also sometimes called the *internet economy*, *new economy*, or *web economy*. Increasingly, the *digital economy* is intertwined with the traditional economy making a clear delineation harder.

In this new economy, digital networking and communication infrastructures provide a global platform over which people and organizations devise strategies, interact, communicate, collaborate and search for information.

It is widely accepted that the growth of the digital economy has widespread impact on the whole economy. Various attempts at categorising the size of the impact on traditional sectors have been made.

Given its expected broad impact, traditional firms are actively assessing how to respond to the changes brought about by the digital economy. For corporations, timing of their response is of the essence. Banks are trying to innovate and use digital tools to improve their traditional business.

12.2.2 Knowledge Economy: Knowledge economy is the use of knowledge to generate tangible and intangible values. Technology and in particular knowledge technology, helps to transform a part of human knowledge to machines. This knowledge can be used by decision support systems in various fields and generate economic values. Knowledge economy is also possible without technology.

Other than the agricultural-intensive economies and labour-intensive economies, the global economy is in transition to a *knowledge economy*, as an extension of an *information society* in information age led by innovations. The transition requires that the rules and practices that determined success in the industrial economy need rewriting in an interconnected, globalized economy where knowledge resources such as trade secrets and expertise are as critical as other economic resources.

A key concept of the knowledge economy is that knowledge and education (often referred to as *human capital*) can be treated as one of the following two:

- A business product, as educational and innovative intellectual products and services can be exported for a high value return.
- A productive asset.

It can be defined as products and services based on knowledge-intensive activities that contribute to an accelerated pace of technical and scientific advance, as well as rapid obsolescence. The key component of a knowledge economy is a greater reliance on intellectual capabilities than on physical inputs or natural resources.

The key problem in the formalization and modelling of knowledge economy is a vague definition of *knowledge*, which is a rather relative concept. For example, it is not proper to consider *information society* as interchangeable with *knowledge society*. *Information* is usually not equivalent to *knowledge*. Their use, as well, depends on individual and group *preferences*.

The knowledge economy is also seen as the latest stage of

development in global economic restructuring. Thus far, the developed world has transitioned from an agricultural economy to industrial economy to post-industrial/mass production economy to knowledge economy. This latest stage has been marked by the upheavals in technological innovations and the globally competitive need for innovation with new products and processes that develop from the research community.

In the knowledge economy, the specialized labour force is characterized as computer literate and well-trained in handling data, developing algorithms and simulated models, and innovating on processes and systems. Consequently, computer scientists, engineers, chemists, biologists, mathematicians, and scientific inventors will see continuous demand in years to come. Hence, knowledge is the catalyst and connective tissue in modern economies.

Knowledge provides the technical expertise, problem-solving, performance measurement and evaluation, and data management needed for the trans-boundary, interdisciplinary global scale of today's competition.

Worldwide examples of the knowledge economy taking place among many others include: Silicon Valley (California, US); aerospace and automotive engineering (Munich, Germany); biotechnology (Hyderabad, India); electronics and digital media (Seoul, South Korea); and petrochemical and energy industry in (Brazil).

It has been suggested that the next evolutionary step after knowledge economy is the network economy, where the relatively localized knowledge is now being shared among and across various networks for the benefit of the network members as a whole.

The knowledge economy has manifold forms in which it may appear but there are predictions that the new economy will extend radically, creating a pattern in which even ideas will be recognised and identified as a commodity. This certainly is not the best time to make any hasty judgment on this contention, but considering the very nature of *knowledge* itself, added to the fact that it is the thrust of this new form of economy, there certainly is a clear way forward for this notion, though the particulars remain in the speculative realm, as of now.

12.3 Digital India (DI): Vision 2019

Digital India is an initiative of the Government of India to integrate Government Ministries/Departments with the people of India. It aims at ensuring the availability of government services to citizens electronically by reducing paperwork. The initiative also includes plans to connect rural areas with high-speed internet networks. DI has three core components. These include creation of digital infrastructure, delivering services digitally and digital literacy.

The project, being handled by the Department of Electronics and Information Technology of the Ministry of Communications and Information Technology, is slated for completion by 2019. A two-way platform will be created where both the service providers and the consumers stand to benefit. The scheme will be monitored and controlled by the *Digital India Advisory Group* which will be chaired by the Ministry of Communications and Information Technology. It is an inter-ministerial initiative where all Ministries and Departments will offer their own services to the public such as healthcare, education, judicial services etc. The public-private-partnership (PPP) model will be adopted selectively. In addition, there are plans to restructure the National Informatics Centre (NIC). This project is one among the top priority projects of Prime Minister Narendra Modi.

The Government of India entity Bharat Broadband Network Limited (BBNL) which executes the National Optical Fibre Network project will be the custodian of DI project. BBNL has ordered United Telecoms Limited to connect 2,50,000 villages through GPON to ensure FTTH based broadband. This will provide the first basic set up to implement DI project.

12.3.1 What is Digital India? Digital India is a programme to transform India into a digitally empowered society and knowledge economy. It has the following components:

1. Digital India is a programme to prepare India for a knowledge future.
2. The focus is on being transformative–to realize IT + IT = IT.
3. The focus is on making technology central to enabling change.
4. It is an Umbrella Programme, covering many departments.

- It weaves together a large number of ideas and thoughts into a single, comprehensive vision so that each of them is seen as part of a larger goal.
- Each individual element stands on its own. But is also part of the larger picture.
- It is coordinated by DeitY, implemented by the entire government.
- The weaving together makes the Mission transformative in totality

5. The Programme:

- Pulls together many existing schemes.
- These schemes will be restructured and re-focused.
- They will be implemented in a synchronized manner.
- Many elements are only process improvements with minimal cost.

6. The common branding of programmes as Digital India highlights their transformative impact.

12.3.2 Vision of Digital India: The Vision of Digital India is cantered on the following 3 key areas:

1. Digital infrastructure as a utility to every citizen.
2. Governance and services on demand.
3. Digital empowerment of citizens.

A. Vision Area 1: Infrastructure as Utility to Every Citizen

- High speed internet as a core utility.
- Cradle to grave digital identity: unique, lifelong, online, authenticable.
- Mobile phone and bank account enabling participation in digital and financial space.

- Easy access to a common service centre.
- Shareable private space on a public cloud.
- Safe and secure cyber space.

B. Vision Area 2: Governance and Services on Demand

- Seamlessly integrated across departments or jurisdictions.
- Services available in real time from online and mobile platform.
- All citizen entitlements to be available on the cloud.
- Services digitally transformed for improving *Ease of Doing Business.*
- Making financial transactions electronic and cashless.
- Leveraging GIS for decision support systems and development.

C. Vision Area 3: Digital Empowerment of Citizens

- Universal digital literacy.
- Universally accessible digital resources.
- All documents/certificates to be available on cloud.
- Availability of digital resources and services in Indian languages.
- Collaborative digital platforms for participative governance.
- Portability of all entitlements through cloud.

12.3.3 Nine Pillars of Digital India

1. Broadband highways.
2. Universal access to phones.
3. Public internet access programme.
4. E-governance–reforming government through technology.
5. eKranti—electronic delivery of services.
6. Information for all.
7. Electronics manufacturing–target NET ZERO imports.
8. IT for jobs.
9. Early harvest programmes.

A. Pillar 1: Broadband Highways

- **Broadband for all Rural Areas**

A. Coverage: 2,50,000 GP.
B. Timeline: December 2016.

C. CAPEX: ₹ 32,000 crore.
D. Nodal Department: DoT.

- **Broadband for all Urban Areas**

A. Virtual network operators for service delivery.
B. Mandate communication infrastructure in new urban development and buildings.

- **National Information Infrastructure**

A. Coverage: Nationwide.
B. Timeline: March 2017.
C. Cost: ₹ 15,686 crore.
D. Nodal Department: DeitY.

B. Pillar 2. Universal Access to Mobile Connectivity

- **Universal Access to Mobile Connectivity**

A. Coverage: Remaining uncovered villages (~42,300 villages).
B. Timeline: 2014-18.
C. Cost: ₹ 16,000 crore.
D. Nodal Department: DoT.

C. Pillar 3. Public Internet Access Programme-National Rural Internet Mission

- **CSCs–Made Viable, Multi-functional End-points for Service Delivery**

A. Coverage: 2,50,000 villages (now 1,30,000).
B. Timeline: 3 Years-March 2017.
C. Cost: ₹ 4,750 crore.
D. Nodal Agency: DeitY.

- **Post Offices to become Multi-Service Centres**

A. Coverage: 1,50,000 post offices.
B. Timeline: 2 Years.
C. Nodal Agency: D/o Posts.

D. Pillar 4: E-governance: Reforming Government through Technology

- **Government Business Process Re-engineering Using IT to Improve Transactions**

A. Form simplification and reduction.
B. Online applications and tracking, and interface between

departments.

C. Use of online repositories, e.g. school certificates, voter ID cards etc.

D. Integration of services and platforms—UIDAI, payment gateway, mobile platform, EDI.

- **Electronic Databases—All databases and information to be electronic, not manual.**
- **Workflow automation inside government.**
- **Public Grievance Redressal—Using IT to automate, respond, analyse data to identify and resolve persistent problems—largely process improvements.**

E. Pillar 5: eKranti—Electronic Delivery of Services

- **Technology for Education—e-Education**

A. All schools connected with broadband.

B. Free wi-fi in all schools (2,50,000).

C. Digital literacy programme.

D. MOOCs (massive online open courses).

- **Technology for Health–e-Healthcare**

A. Online medical consultation.

B. Online medical records.

C. Online medicine supply.

D. Pan-India exchange for patient information.

E. Pilots: 2015; Full coverage in 3 years.

- **Technology for Planning**

A. GIS-based decision-making.

B. National GIS Mission Mode Project.

- **Technology for Farmers**

A. Real time price information.

B. Online ordering of inputs.

C. Online cash, loan, relief payment with mobile banking.

- **Technology for Security**

A. Mobile emergency services.

- **Technology for Financial Inclusion**

A. Mobile banking.

B. Micro ATM programme.

C. CSCs/post offices.

- **Technology for Justice**

A. e-Courts, e-Police, e- Jails, e-Prosecution.

- **Technology for Security**

A. National Cyber Security Co-ordination Centre.

F. Pillar 6: Information for All

- **Online Hosting of Information and Documents**

A. Citizens have open, easy access to information.

B. Open data platform.

- **Government Pro-actively Engages through Social Media and Web-based Platforms to Inform Citizens**

A. MyGov.in.

B. 2-way communication between citizens and government.

- **Online Messaging to Citizens on Special Occasions and Programmes**
- **Largely Utilise Existing Infrastructure: Limited Additional Resources Needed**

G. Pillar 7: Electronics Manufacturing: Target *Net Zero* Imports by 2020

- **Target *Net Zero* Imports is a Striking Demonstration of Intent**
- **Ambitious Goal which Requires Co-ordinated Action on Many Fronts**

A. Taxation, incentives.

B. Economies of scale, eliminate cost disadvantages.

C. Focused areas—big ticket items (FABS, Fab-less design, Set top boxes, VSATs, mobiles, consumer and medical electronics, smart energy meters, smart cards, micro ATMs

D. Incubators, clusters.

E. Skill development.

F. Government procurement.

H. Pillar 8: IT for Jobs

- **Train People in Smaller Towns and Villages for IT Sector Jobs**

A. Coverage: 1 crore students.

B. Timeline: 5 years.

C. Cost: ₹ 200 crore for weaker sections.

D. Nodal Agency: DeitY.

- **IT/ITES in North-East**

A. Scope: Setting up of BPO per NE State.
B. Coverage: NE States.
C. Nodal Agency: DeitY.

- **Train Service Delivery Agents to Run Viable Businesses Delivering IT Services**

A. Coverage: 3,00,000.
B. Timeline: 2 Years.
C. Nodal Agency: DeitY.

- **Telecom Service Providers to Train Rural Workforce to Cater to Their Own Needs**

A. Coverage: 5,00,000.
B. Timeline: 5 Years.
C. Nodal Agency: DoT.

I. Pillar 9: Early Harvest Programmes

- **IT Platform for Messages**

A. Coverage: Elected representatives, all Government employees.
B. 1.36 crore mobiles and 22 lakh emails.
C. Mass messaging application developed.

- **Government Greetings to be e-Greetings**

A. Basket of e-Greetings templates available.
B. Crowd sourcing of e-Greetings thru MyGov.
C. e-Greetings portal ready by August 14, 2014.

- **Biometric Attendance**

A. Coverage: All Central Government Offices in Delhi.
B. Operational in DeitY and initiated in urban development.
C. On-boarding started in other departments.
D. Procurement of devices—tender issued.

- **Wi-fi in All Universities**

A. Scope: All universities on NKN.
B. 400 additional universities.
C. Cost: ₹ 790 crore.

- **Secure E-mail within Government**

A. Phase I upgradation for 10 lakh employees done.
B. Phase II for 50 lakh employees by March 2015.

C. Cost: ₹ 98 crore.

- **Standardize Government email design**

A. Standardised templates under preparation.

- **Public Wi-fi Hotspots**

A. Coverage: Cities with population >1 million, tourist centres.

B. Nodal Agency: DoT/MoUD.

- **School Books to be e-Books**

A. Nodal Agency: MHRD/DeitY.

- **SMS-based Weather Information, Disaster Alerts**

A. DeitY's Mobile Seva Platform ready.

B. Nodal Agency: MoES (IMD)/MHA (NDMA).

- **National Portal for Lost and Found Children**

A. Nodal Agency: DeitY/DoWCD.

12.3.4 Estimated Cost

- **Overall Costs of Digital India**

  ₹ 1,00,000 crore in ongoing schemes.

  ₹ 13,000 crore for new schemes and activities.

12.3.5 Impact of Digital India by 2019

- Broadband in 2.5 lakh villages, and universal phone connectivity.
- Net zero imports by 2020.
- 4,00,000 public internet access points.
- Wi-fi in 2.5 lakh schools, all universities; Public wi-fi hotspots for citizens.
- Digital Inclusion: 1.7 crore trained for IT, telecom and electronics jobs.
- Job creation: direct 1.7 crore and indirect at least 8.5 crore.
- E-governance and e-Services: Across Government.
- India to be leader in IT use in services—health, education, banking.
- Digitally-empowered citizens—public cloud, internet access.

12.3.6 Challenges and Changes Needed

- Programme on this scale never conceived.
- Each pillar/programme has own challenges.

- Human resource issues.

A. NIC-not equipped for a fraction of this task (obsolescence)—needs revamping and restructuring.
B. DeitY—needs programme managers—at least 4 more officers at senior levels.
C. Ministries—need a chief information officer/chief technology officer.

- **Financial Resources Issues**

A. Mostly structured around ongoing programmes: Better focus, need some restructuring.
B. Some others are process improvements or better utilisation of resources.
C. A few new programmes may be needed, particularly in electronics manufacturing and skill development.

- **Co-ordination Issues**

A. Programme covers many other departments.
B. Need commitment and effort.
C. Leadership and support critical for success.

12.3.7 Digital India (DI): A Critique: DI initiative is a promising initiative of the Indian Government. Many companies have shown their interest in this project. However, it is not free from challenges and legal hurdles. Some believe that DI cannot be successful till mandatory e-governance services are introduced in India. Incomplete implementation of the National e-Governance Plan of India will also adversely affect the success of the DI project. India has poor regulations in the field of privacy protection, data protection, cyber laws, telegraph, e-governance, e-commerce etc. Further, many legal experts believe that e-governance and DI without cyber security are useless. The cyber security trends in India have exposed the vulnerability of Indian cyberspace. Even the National Cyber Security Policy, 2013, has not been implemented till now. In these circumstances, critical infrastructure protection would be a tough task to manage for the Indian Government. The project also lacks the concept of proper e-waste management.

DI initiatives would be required to comply with the civil

liberties requirements in general and civil liberties protection in cyberspace in particular. India has not given any importance to privacy and privacy laws so far. Indian Government indulges into mass surveillance in India and projects like Aadhaar, and Central Monitoring System are operating without any law and parliamentary oversight. The intelligence agencies of India like Intelligence Bureau (IB) and law enforcement agencies like Central Bureau of Investigation (CBI) are operating for decades without any law and parliamentary scrutiny. DI would further strengthen the mass surveillance activities of the Indian Government if proper procedural safeguards are not implemented and practiced.

The initiative is commendable and deserves full support of all stakeholders. Nevertheless, the initiative lacks some crucial components including inadequate legal framework, absence of privacy and data protection laws, possibilities of civil liberties abuse, lack of parliamentary oversight for e-surveillance, lack of intelligence-related reforms, insecure Indian cyberspace etc. These issues have to be addressed for successful planning and implementation of DI initiative. Still, DI project is worth exploring and implementation despite its shortcomings that can be rectified before/during its implementation.

If correctly implemented, Digital India project can change the way public services would be delivered in India in the near future.

13

Crypto Currency: Dangers and Remedial Measures

13.1 What is Crypto Currency?

Crypto currency is a class of privately issued digital means of payment that depends predominantly on cryptography and distributed ledger technology (DLT) such as the block chain. A block chain is a continuous ledger in which transactions are stored as blocks and linked using cryptography. Crypto currency is often allotted through initial coin offerings (ICOs), which are used as a means of raising capital through crowd-funding. Crypto currency typically has some monetary characteristics, but is not a liability of any entity and is not backed by any authority. Its value is driven by users' confidence in it. This, coupled with limited supply, makes its value highly volatile and, therefore, not a reliable medium of exchange or store of value.

13.2 Dangers Posed by Crypto Currency

Though crypto currency may not currently pose systemic risks, its increasing popularity leading to price bubbles raises serious concerns for consumer and investor protection, and market integrity.

The crypto currency eco-system may affect the existing payment and settlement system which could, in turn, influence the transmission of monetary policy. Furthermore, being stored in digital/electronic media—electronic wallets—it is prone to hacking and operational risk, a few instances of which have already been observed globally. There is no established framework for recourse to customer problems and disputes resolution as payments by crypto currencies take place on a peer-to-peer basis without an authorised central agency which regulates such payments. There exists a high possibility of its usage for illicit activities, including tax avoidance.

The absence of information on counterparties in such peer-to-peer anonymous or pseudonymous systems could subject users to unintentional breaches of anti-money laundering laws as well as laws for combating the financing of terrorism. A globally coordinated approach is necessary to prevent abuses and to strictly limit interconnections with regulated financial institutions.

13.3 Remedial Measures

On a global level, regulatory responses to crypto currency have ranged from a complete *clamp down* in some jurisdictions to a comparatively *light touch regulatory approach*. The Securities and Exchange Commission (SEC) and the Commodity Futures Trading Commission (CFTC) have emerged as the primary regulators of crypto currencies in the United States, where these assets like most other jurisdictions, do not enjoy the legal tender status. Asian countries have experienced oversized concentration of crypto players. Thus, Japan and South Korea account for the biggest shares of crypto asset markets in the world. In the case of Bit coins, half of transactions worldwide are carried out in Japan. In September 2017, Japan approved transactions by its exchanges in crypto currencies. China's exchanges hosted disproportionately large volumes of global Bit coin trading until their ban recently.

In India, the Government and the Reserve Bank of India (RBI) are keeping a close watch on crypto currency and have issued pre-emptive cautionary warnings. In early April 2018, RBI barred its regulated entities from dealing in or providing services to any individual or business entities dealing with or settling in virtual currencies. Regulated entities which already provide such services were asked to exit the relationship within 3 months.

Developments on this front need to be monitored as some trading may shift from exchanges to peer-to-peer mode, which may also involve increased usage of cash. Possibilities of migration of crypto exchange houses to dark pools/cash and to offshore locations, thus raising concerns on money laundering as well as financing of terrorism.

Rapid changes in the landscape of the payments industry, along with factors such as emergence of private digital tokens and the rising costs of managing fiat paper/metallic money, have led central banks around the world to explore the option of introducing fiat digital currencies. In India, an inter-departmental group has been constituted by RBI to study and provide guidance on the desirability and feasibility to introduce a central bank digital currency.

In his Budget Speech to the Parliament on February 1, 2018, Finance Minister Shri Arun Jaitley observed, "Distributed ledger system or the block chain technology allows organization of any chain of records or transactions without the need of intermediaries. The Government does not consider crypto-currencies legal tender or coin and will take all measures to eliminate use of these crypto assets in financing illegitimate activities or as part of the payment system. The Government will explore use of block chain technology proactively for ushering in digital economy". [1]

In July 2018, RBI banned all banks, non-banking financial companies (NBFCs) and other financial institutions from crypto transactions.

Though crypto currency is not a legal tender yet it is not illegal for Indians to buy, own or sell bitcoins. Unlike regular currency which has government backing, crypto currency one can hold at once own risk. In October 2018, crypto currency exchange Unocoin launched an ATM (or a kiosk) in Bengaluru for Indians to buy and sell bitcoins. However, it was soon closed by the authorities for being illegal and without approval.

Endnote

1. Government of India, Ministry of Finance, Budget Papers 2018-19, *Speech of the Finance Minister*, para 112.

14

India's Cyber Security Policy

Information technology (IT) is one of the critical sectors that rides on and resides in cyber space. It has emerged as one of the most significant growth catalysts for the Indian economy. In addition to fuelling India's economy, this sector is also positively influencing the lives of the people through direct and indirect contribution to the various socio-economic parameters such as employment, standard of living and diversity among others. The sector has played a significant role in transforming India's image to that of a global player in providing world-class technology solutions and IT business services. The government has been a key driver for increases adoption of IT-based products and IT-enabled services.

14.1 What is Cyber Space?

Cyber space is a complex environment consisting of interactions between people, software and services, supported by worldwide distribution of information and communication technology (ICT) devices and networks.

Owing to the numerous benefits brought about by technological advancements, the cyber space is a common pool used by citizens, businesses, critical information infrastructure, military and governments in a manner that makes it difficult to draw clear boundaries among these different groups. The cyber space is expected to be more complex in the foreseeable future, with many-fold increase in networks and devices connected to it.

14.2 Need for Cyber Security

Cyber space is vulnerable to a wide variety of incidents, whether intentional or accidental, man-made or natural, and the data exchanged in the cyber space can be exploited for nefarious purposes by both nation-states and non-state actors. Cyber attacks that target the infrastructure or underlying economic well-being of a nation-state can effectively reduce available state resources and undermine confidence in their supporting structures. A cyber related incident of national significance may take any form: an organized cyber attack, an uncontrolled exploit such as computer virus or worms or any malicious software code, a national disaster with significant cyber consequences or other related incidents capable of causing extensive damage to the information infrastructure or key assets. Large-scale cyber incidents may overwhelm the government, public and private sector resources and services by disrupting functioning of critical information systems. Complications from disruption of such a magnitude may threaten lives, economy and national security.

Rapid identification, information exchange, investigation and co-ordinated response and remediation can mitigate the damage caused by malicious cyber space activity. Some of the examples of cyber threats to individuals, businesses and government are identity theft, phishing, social engineering, activism, cyber terrorism, compound threats targeting mobile devices and smart phone, compromised digital certificates, advanced persistent threats, denial of service, bot nets, supply chain attacks, and data leakages.

14.3 National Cyber Security Policy (NCSP), 2013

NCSP was a policy framework by Department of Electronics and Information Technology (DeitY), Ministry of Communication and Information Technology, Government of India. It aimed at protecting the public and private infrastructure from cyber attacks. The policy also intended to safeguard "information, such as personal information (of web users), financial and banking information and sovereign data". This was particularly relevant in the wake of US National Security Agency (NSA) leaks that suggested the US government agencies are spying on Indian users, who have no legal or technical safeguards against it. Ministry of Communications and Information Technology (India) defined cyber space as a complex environment consisting of interactions between people, software services supported by worldwide distribution of information and communication technology.

India had no Cyber security policy before 2013. In 2013, *The Hindu* newspaper, citing documents leaked by NSA whistle blower Edward Snowden, has alleged that much of the NSA surveillance was focused on India's domestic politics and its strategic and commercial interests. This leads to spark furore among people. Under pressure, Government unveiled a National Cyber Security Policy 2013 on July 2, 2013.

Vision: To build a secure and resilient cyberspace for citizens, business and government.

Mission: To protect information and information infrastructure in cyberspace, build capabilities to prevent and respond to cyber threat, reduce vulnerabilities and minimize damage from cyber incidents through a combination of institutional structures, people, processes, technology and cooperation.

14.3.1 Objectives of NCSP: These are as under:

1. To create a secure cyber ecosystem in the country, generate adequate trust and confidence in IT system and transactions in cyberspace and thereby enhance adoption of IT in all sectors of the economy.
2. To create an assurance framework for design of security policies and promotion and enabling actions for compliance to global security standards and best practices by way of conformity assessment (product, process, technology and people).
3. To strengthen the regulatory framework for ensuring a secure cyberspace ecosystem.
4. To enhance and create national and sectoral level 24x7 mechanism for obtaining strategic information regarding threats to ICT infrastructure, creating scenarios for response, resolution and crisis management through effective

predictive, preventive, protective response and recovery actions.

5. To enhance the protection and resilience of nation's critical information infrastructure by operating a 24x7 National Critical Information Infrastructure Protection Centre (NCIIPC) and mandating security practices related to the design, acquisition, development, use and operation of information resources.
6. To develop suitable indigenous security technologies through frontier technology research, solution-oriented research, proof of concept, pilot development, transition, diffusion and commercialization leading to widespread deployment of secure ICT products/processes in general and specifically for addressing national security requirements.
7. To improve visibility of integrity of ICT products and services by establishing infrastructure for testing and validation of security of such product.
8. To create work force for 5,00,000 professionals skilled in next 5 years through capacity building, skill development and training.
9. To provide fiscal benefit to businesses for adoption of standard security practices and processes.
10. To enable protection of information while in process, handling, storage and transit so as to safeguard privacy of citizen's data and reducing economic losses due to cyber crime or data theft.
11. To enable effective prevention, investigation and prosecution of cyber crime and enhancement of law enforcement capabilities through appropriate legislative intervention.
12. To create a culture of cyber security and privacy enabling responsible user behaviour and actions through an effective communication and promotion strategy.
13. To develop effective public-private-partnerships and collaborative engagements through technical and operational co-operation and contribution for enhancing the security of cyber space.

14. To enhance global co-operation by promoting shared understanding and leveraging relationships for furthering the cause of security of cyber space.

14.3.2 Strategies of NCSP:

1. Creating a secure cyber ecosystem.
2. Creating an assurance framework.
3. Encouraging open standards.
4. Strengthening the regulatory framework.
5. Creating mechanism for security threat early warning, vulnerability management and response to security threats.
6. Securing e-governance services.
7. Protection and resilience of critical information infrastructure.
8. Promotion of research and development in cyber security.
9. Reducing supply chain risks
10. Human resources development.
11. Creating cyber security awareness.
12. Developing effective public-private-partnership (PPP).
13. Information sharing and co-operation.
14. Prioritized approach for implementation.

A. Creating a Secure Cyber Ecosystem:

- To designate a national nodal agency to co-ordinate all matters related to cyber security in the country, with clearly defined roles and responsibilities.
- To encourage all organizations, private and public to designate a member of senior management as chief information security officer (CISO), responsible for cyber security efforts and initiatives.
- To encourage all organizations to develop information security policies duly integrated with their business plans and implement such policies as per international best practices. Such policies should include establishing standards and mechanisms for secure information flow, crisis management plan, proactive security posture assessment and forensically-enabled information infrastructure.

- To ensure that all organizations earmark a specific budget for implementing cyber security initiatives and for meeting emergency response arising out of cyber incidents.
- To provide fiscal schemes and incentives to encourage entities to install, strengthen and upgrade information infrastructure with respect to cyber security.
- To prevent occurrence and recurrence of cyber incidents by way of incentives for technology development, cyber security compliance and proactive actions.
- To establish a mechanism for sharing information and for identifying and responding to cyber security incidents and for co-operation in restoration efforts.
- To encourage entities to adopt guidelines for procurement of trustworthy ICT products and provide for procurement of indigenously manufactured ICT products that have security implications.

B. Creating an Assurance Framework:

- To promote adoption of global best practices in information security and compliance and thereby enhance cyber security posture.
- To create infrastructure for conformity assessment and certification of compliance to cyber security best practices, and standards and guidelines.
- To enable implementation of global security best practices in formal risk assessment and risk management processes, business continuity management and cyber crisis management plan by all entities within Government and in critical sectors, to reduce the risk of disruption and improve the security posture.
- To identify and classify information infrastructure facilities and assets at entity level with respect to risk perception for undertaking commensurate security protection measures.
- To encourage secure application/software development processes based on global best practices.
- To create conformity assessment framework for periodic verification of compliance to best practices, standards and

guidelines on cyber security.

- To encourage all entities to periodically test and evaluate the adequacy and effectiveness of technical and operational security control measures implemented in IT systems and in networks.

C. Encouraging Open Standards:

- To encourage use of open standards to facilitate interoperability and data exchange among different products and services.
- To promote a consortium of Government and private sector to enhance the availability of tested and certified IT products based on open standards.

D. Strengthening the Regulatory Framework:

- To develop a dynamic legal framework and its periodic review to address the cyber security challenges arising out of technological developments in cyber space and its harmonization with international frameworks including those related to internet governance.
- To mandate periodic audit and evaluation of the adequacy and effectiveness of security of information infrastructure as may be appropriate, with respect to regulatory framework.
- To enable, educate and facilitate awareness of the regulatory framework.

E. Creating Mechanism for Security Threat Early Warning, Vulnerability Management and Response to Security Threats:

- To create national level systems, processes, structures and mechanisms to generate necessary situational scenario of existing and potential cyber security threats and enable timely information sharing for proactive, preventing and protective actions by individual entities.
- To operate a 24x7 National Level Computer Emergency Response Team (CERT) to function as a nodal agency for co-ordination of all efforts for cyber security emergency response and crisis management.
- To operationalize 24x7 sectoral CERTs for all co-

ordination and communication actions within the respective sectors for effective incidence response and resolution and cyber crisis management.

- To implement Cyber Crisis Management Plan for dealing with cyber related incidents impacting critical national processes or endangering public safety and security of the nation, by way of well co-ordinated multi-disciplinary approach at the national sectoral as well as entity levels.
- To conduct and facilitate regular cyber security drills and exercises at national, sectoral and entity levels to enable assessment of the security posture and level of emergency preparedness in resisting and dealing with cyber security incidents.

F. Securing E-governance Services:

- To mandate implementation of global security best practices, business continuity management and cyber crisis management plan for all e-governance initiatives in the country, to reduce the risk of disruption and improve the security posture.
- To encourage wider usage of public key infrastructure (PKI) within government for trusted communication and transactions.
- To engage information security professionals and organizations to assist e-governance initiatives and ensure conformance to security best practices.

G. Protection and Resilience of Critical Information Infrastructure:

- To develop a plan for protection of critical information infrastructure and its integration with business plan at the entity level and implement such plan. The plans shall include establishing mechanisms for secure information flow, guidelines and standards, crisis management plan, proactive security posture assessment and forensically-enabled information infrastructure.
- To operate a 24x7 National Critical Information Infrastructure Protection Centre (NCIIPC) to function as

the nodal agency for critical information infrastructure protection in the country.

- To facilitate identification, prioritisation, assessment, remediation and protection of critical infrastructure and key resources based on the plan for protection of critical information infrastructure.
- To mandate implementation of global security best practices, business continuity management and cyber crisis management plan by all critical sector entities, to reduce the risk of disruption and improve the security posture.
- To encourage and mandate as appropriate, the use of validated and certified IT products.
- To mandate security audit of critical information infrastructure on a periodic basis.
- To mandate certification for all security roles to those involved in operation of critical information infrastructure.
- To mandate secure application/software development process based on global best practices.

H. Promotion of Research and Development in Cyber Security:

- To undertake research and development programmes for addressing all aspects of development aimed at short-term, medium-term and long-term goals which include development of trustworthy systems, their testing, deployment and maintenance throughout the life cycle.
- To encourage research and development to produce cost-effective, tailor-made indigenous security solutions meeting a wider range of cyber security challenges and target for export markets.
- To facilitate transition, diffusion and commercialization of the outputs of research and development into commercial products and services for use in public and private sectors.
- To set up centres of excellence in areas of strategic importance for the point of security of cyber space.
- To collaborate in joint research and development projects with industry and academia in frontline technologies and

solution-oriented research.

I. Reducing Supply Chain Risks:

- To create and maintain testing infrastructure and facilities for IT security product evaluation and compliance verification as per global standards and practices.
- To build trusted relationships with product/system vendors and service providers for improving end-to-end supply chain security visibility.
- To create awareness of the threats, vulnerabilities and consequences of breach of security among entities for managing supply chain risks related to IT (products, systems or services) procurement.

J. Human Resources Development:

- To foster education and training programmes both in formal and informal sectors to support the nation's cyber security needs and build capacity.
- To establish cyber security training infrastructure across the country by way of public-private-partnership arrangements.
- To establish cyber security concept labs for awareness and skill development in key areas.
- To establish institutional mechanisms for capacity building for law enforcement agencies.

K. Creating Cyber Security Awareness:

- To promote and launch a comprehensive national awareness programme on security of cyber space.
- To sustain security literacy awareness and publicity campaign through electronic media to help citizens to be aware of the challenges of cyber security.
- To conduct, support and enable cyber security workshops/seminars and certifications.

L. Developing Effective Public-Private-Partnership (PPP):

- To facilitate collaboration and co-operation among stakeholder entities including private sector, in the area of cyber security in general and protection of critical information infrastructure in particular for actions related to cyber threats, vulnerabilities, breaches, potential protective measures, and adoption of best practices.

- To create models for collaborations and engagements with all relevant stakeholders.
- To create a think tank for cyber security policy inputs, discussion and deliberations.

M. Information Sharing and Co-operation:

- To develop bilateral and multilateral relationships in the area of cyber security with other countries.
- To enhance national and global co-operation among security agencies, defence agencies and forces, law enforcement agencies and judicial systems.
- To create mechanisms for dialogue related to technical and operational aspects with industry in order to facilitate efforts in recovery and resilience of systems including critical information infrastructure.

N. Prioritized Approach for Implementation:

- To adopt a prioritized approach to implement the policy so as to address the most critical areas in the first instance.

15

Future Perspectives

The efficiency of the financial infrastructure of which the payments and settlement process is a crucial component, is an important factor in promoting financial sector development, in improving the effectiveness of monetary policy, and in reducing the country risk profile. Integration of the payments services across the country and markets abroad is an important reason for improving the payments system.

The experience of computerisation of clearing operations as well as the small beginnings in electronic payments and electronic banking has revealed the need for expansion and upgradation of technology. Still, the development of the payments system is not just a matter of technology. It requires high availability of reliable communication network, the integration of work processes, and delivery systems.

The payment instruments are constantly changing and newer products and services are being innovated in the developed and developing countries and these are being introduced with suitable modifications and safeguards in India. At the retail level a wide range of payment instruments are catering to the needs of different types of economic transactions. At the level of inter-bank payments and settlements, real time and on-line funds transfer are likely to play a major role both in local as well as inter-city dealings.

The spread and the reach of the modern system should enable equal and convenient access from both small and big centres alike. The design of an integrated system should be such that there is a wide choice of payments instruments at the retail level and there is end-to-end connectivity over all parts of the country to enable delivery of these instruments through fast, reliable and secure communications.

An integrated system would enable real time movement of funds between different financial markets, allow fair and equal access to all the financial intermediaries and enable effective regulatory oversight. The fundamental requirement is the integration of various payments instruments, transactions and settlements into a single system which combines flexibility with efficiency. This would have implications for not merely seigniorage but also the conduct of monetary policy.

Governments will continue to prioritise improving standard e-payment services, such as tax payments/refunds and pension contributions, over other services. They will also focus on enhancing one-stop shops with, for example, more powerful search engines and more intuitive interfaces. Welfare payments will also be increasingly digitalised, partly as a means to ensure financial inclusion among poorer segments of the population.

Technological infrastructure will develop rapidly, underpinning the evolution of novel processes. Within the next few years, many around the world will likely be connected to the imminent 5G networks—CCS Insight, a research house, expects 1 billion users by 2023, half of whom will be in China. These networks promise speeds ten times faster than today's 4G networks, and much bigger data capacities that will pave the way for, among other things, augmented- and virtual-reality technologies, driverless cars, and numerous other sensors around smart cities communicating with one another as part of the internet of things. If the recent advent of checkout-free stores is any indication, e-payments will become even more seamless.

Managing data security and privacy will remain a priority for policymakers. Given varying degrees of discomfort with government surveillance around the world, different jurisdictions will approach regulation in different ways. This could lead to some regulatory arbitrage as fintechs seek out less onerous regulatory regimes. The more radical e-payment innovations—for instance, those incorporating facial recognition technology—could emerge in countries such as China, where citizens seem to be more tolerant of potential privacy intrusions.

The global e-payments ecosystem will continue to evolve at a staggering pace, as traditional concepts of finance, personal identity and trust are upended almost overnight by technological advances. Governments have been trying to strike a balance between e-payments' promise—for instance, increased efficiency in tax collection and social services expenditure—and their possible risks.

Like consumers, governments can choose whether or not to participate in e-payments, as either a payer or a payee. As a payer, the government is a buyer of services and goods and thus needs to pay its suppliers; the government also transfers money to its residents, businesses and institutions, as well as to other governments. As a payee, the government receives payments from those parties. Given the significant size of the public sector in most countries, the opportunity for governments to participate in and influence e-payments is sizeable.

Consumers in the least developed countries (as well as in developed ones) are becoming ever more comfortable with having touch screen computers in their pockets—and are constantly finding new and novel ways to use them, not least in their efforts to make payments through more convenient and secure digital methods.

Providers of e-payment services are part of a burgeoning industry now known as fintech—where technology enables financial services—which purports to alter traditional financial business models through the use of modern technology. Fintech firms provide services in digital payments, investments, financing, insurance, advisory services, security and much more. Despite some early worries about inadequate consumer protection from unregulated fintech services, governments are increasingly seizing opportunities to work with fintech firms. A collaborative approach among fintech firms, governments and the traditional financial services industry will serve to mitigate potential drawbacks caused by disruption of the financial industry (for example, harming consumers or causing inefficient allocation of capital). Such an approach will also encourage innovation and promote the benefits of fintech (for example, faster provision of financial services, including digital payments adoption).

It is no surprise, then, that many emerging-market countries are altering their digital payment growth trajectories thanks to mobile payments.

For many in emerging-market countries, their first experience of finance may be through a mobile phone, rather than at a bricks-and-mortar bank branch. In terms of e-payments, emerging markets, which are not burdened by legacy systems, habits and business processes, are the beneficiaries of two simultaneous kinds of leapfrogging (financial and technological), by adopting the latest products in digital finance through the latest technologies.

At a broader global level, government e-payment systems are benefiting from a more customer-centric approach to public service delivery in tandem with a "whole of government" approach. This philosophy seeks to break down silos and integrate cross-ministerial functions in public service management. This has led, among many other things, to an emphasis on digital "one-stop shops", as well as to a far more collaborative and participatory approach to policy implementation and service delivery, even in ostensibly authoritarian states.

While governments around the world are making great strides in enhancing their e-payment systems, the benchmarks and standards against which they are judged are being raised because of relentless technological and behavioural change.

For e-payments, as with many other new technologies, governments around the world have a responsibility to foster an environment in which citizens, businesses and other stakeholders can feel confident experimenting with and adopting new behaviours and processes. This category examines this enabling environment by assessing ten indicators grouped in three buckets: operating environment, trust and safety, and inclusiveness.

Consumers in locations ranging from the least developed to

the most developed countries are becoming ever more comfortable with having touch screen computers in their pockets and are constantly finding new and novel ways to use them—not least in their efforts to make payments through more convenient and secure digital methods.

These forces have changed finance and technology in ways few could have predicted. What seemed futuristic a couple of decades ago is pedestrian now.

Governments, private sector firms and non-governmental organisations, sensing that traditional banking models are evolving and disintermediated, are competing and collaborating in equal measure as they vie for influence in this new age of digital finance.

Bibliography

Bibliography

Arora, A. and S. Athreye (2002), "The Software Industry and India's Economics Development", *Information Economics and Policy,* 14(2), 253-273.

Arora, A., V. S. Arunachalam, J. Asundi and F. Ronald (2001), "The Indian Software Services Industry", *Research Policy*, 30(8), 1267-1287.

Athreye, S. (2003), "The Indian Software Industry and its Evolving Service Capability", Working Paper, The Open University, Walton Hall, Milton Keynes, UK.

Athreye, S. (2005), "The Indian Software Industry", in Arora and Gambardella (eds.), 'From Underdogs to Tigers', Oxford University Press: Oxford.

Balakrishnan, P. (2006), "Benign Neglect or Strategic Intent? Contested Lineage of Indian Software Industry", *Economic and Political Weekly*, Vol. 41, No. 36 September 9.

Balasubramanyam, V. and A. Balasubramanyam (2000), "The Software Cluster in Bangalore", in Dunning (ed.), 'Regions, Globalization and the Knowledge-based Economy', Oxford University Press: Oxford.

Basant, Rakesh and Brian Fikkert (1996), "The Effects of R&D, Foreign Technology Purchase, and Domestic and International Spillovers on Productivity in Indian Firms", *Review of Economics and Statistics* 78(2), 187-200.

Bhattacharya, M. (2004), "Telecom Sector in India: Vision 2020", in 'India Vision 2020', The Report of the Committee on India Vision 2020, Planning Commission, Government of India and Background Papers, Academic Foundation: New Delhi.

Chandrasekhar C.P., Jayati Ghosh and Anamitra Roychowdhury (2006), "The Demographic Dividend and Young India's Economic Future", *Economic and Political Weekly*, Vol. 41, No. 49.

Chandrasekhar, C.P. (2006), "The Political Economy of IT-Driven Outsourcing", in Govindan Parayil (ed.), 'Political Economy and Information Capitalism in India: Digital Divide, Development Divide and Equity', Palgrave Macmillan.

Department of Information Technology (1996), "Guide to

Electronics Industry in India", Department of Information Technology, New Delhi.

Dossani, R. and M. Kenney (2002), "Creating an Environment for Venture Capital in India", *World Development,* 30(2), 227-253.

Dunning, J. (1992), "The Competitive Advantages of Countries and the Activities of Transnational Corporations", *Economist,* Innovative India, April 3, 65-66.

Espenshade, Thomas J. (1999), "High-End Immigrants and the Shortage of Skilled Labour", *Population Research and Policy Review,* 20-135-141, Kluwer Academic Publisher: Netherlands.

Government of India, Ministry of Finance, *Economic Survey* (various years).

Government of India, Planning Commission, *Twelfth Five Year Plan* (2012-17).

Hasan, Rana (2002), "The Impact of Imported and Domestic Technologies on the Productivity of Firms: Panel Data Evidence from Indian Manufacturing Firms", *Journal of Development Economics,* 69(1), 23-49.

Heeks, R. (1996), "India's Software Industry: State Policy, Liberalization and Industrial Development", Sage Publications: New Delhi, Thousand Oaks, London.

Hugo, Graeme (2003), "Migration and Development: A Perspective from Asia", Paper prepared for the International Organization for Migration.

Joseph, K.J. (2006), "Information Technology, Innovation System and Trade Regime in Developing Countries: India and the ASEAN", Palgrave Macmillan: London.

Joseph, K.J. (1997), "Industry Under Economic Liberalization: The Case of Indian Electronics", Sage Publications: New Delhi, Thousand Oaks, London.

Joseph, K.J. and Vinoj Abraham (2007), "Information Technology and Productivity: Evidence from India's Manufacturing Sector", Working Paper No. 389, Centre for Development Studies, Trivandrum.

Joshi, V. (1999), "India's Economic Reforms: 1991-2001", South Asia Books: New Delhi.

Kamibayashi, Cheko (2006), "Current Migration of IT Engineers to Japan: Beyond Immigration Control and Cultural Barriers", in Christiane Kuptsch and Pang Eng Fong (eds.), 'Competing for Global Talent', ILO and ILLS, Geneva.

Kelkar, V., Chaturvedi, D. and Dar, M. (1991), "India's Information Economy: Role, Size and Scope", *Economic and Political Weekly*, September 14, 2153-2160.

Khadria, Binod (1999), "The Migration of Knowledge Workers: Second Generation Effects of India's Brain Drain", Sage Publications: New Delhi.

Khadria, Binod (2001), "Shifting Paradigms of Globalization: The Twenty-first Century Transition towards Generics in Skilled Migration from India", *International Migration*, Vol. 39(5), Special Issue 1.

Kraemer, K.L. and J. Dedrick (2001), "Information Technology and Economic Development: Results and Policy Implications of Cross-Country Studies", in M. Pohjola (ed.), 'Information Technology, Productivity and Economic Growth', Oxford University Press.

Kripalani, M. and P. Engardio (2003), "The Rise of India", *Business Week*, December 8.

Kumar, N. and K.J. Joseph (2005), "Export of Software and Business Process Outsourcing from Developing Countries: Lessons from India", *Asia Pacific Trade and Investment Review* 1(1), 91-108.

Kumar, Nagesh and Aradhna Aggarwal (2005), "Liberalization, Outward Orientation and In-House R&D Activity of Multinational and Local Firms: A Quantitative Exploration for Indian Manufacturing", *Research Policy* 34(4), 441-460.

Lal, K. (1999), "Determinants of the Adoption of Information Technology: A Case Study of Electrical and Electronic goods Manufacturing Firms in India", *Research Policy* 28(7), 667-680.

Mani, S. (2005), "The Dragon vs. the Elephant: Comparative Analysis of Innovation Capability in the Telecommunications Equipment Industry in India and China", Working Paper No. 373, Centre for Development Studies, Trivandrum.

NASSCOM (2006), "Study on Domestic Services (IT-ITES) Market Opportunity", National Association of Software and Science Components (Nasscom), New Delhi.

NASSCOM (2006), "The IT Software and Services Industry in India: Strategic Review, 2004", New Delhi: National Association of Software and Service Companies.

Panagariya, Arvind (2002), "India's Economic Reforms: What Has Been Accomplished? What Remains to be Done?", ERD Policy Brief Series, Economics and Research Department, Asian

Development Bank.

Parthasarathi, A., and K. Joseph (2002), "Limits to Innovation in India's ICT Sector", *Science, Technology and Society*, 7(1), 13-50.

Parthasarthy, B. (2006), "The Political Economy of Indian Software Industry", in Parayil G. (ed.), 'Political Economy and Information Capitalism in India: Digital Divide and Equity', Palgrave Macmillan: New York.

Pohjola, M. (2001), "Information Technology and Economic Growth: A Cross-country Analysis", in M. Pohjola (ed.), 'Information Technology, Productivity and Economic Growth', Oxford University Press: New York.

Raut, Lakshmi K. (1995), "R&D Spillover and Productivity Growth: Evidence from Indian Private Firms", *Journal of Development Economics* 48(1), 1-23.

Sen, S. and F. Frankel (eds.) (2005), "India's Strategy of IT-led Growth", Centre for the Advanced Study of India: Philadelphia, PA.

World Bank (2005), "Project Appraisal Document for an ICT Development", Hanoi, Vietnam.

Websites

Ministry of Finance, Government of India

Ministry of Communications and Information Technology

Reserve Bank of India

National Payments Corporation of India

NITI Aayog

Index

Index